MACHIAVELLI AND US

MACHIAVELLI AND US

LOUIS ALTHUSSER

VERSO
London • New York

This book is supported by the French Ministry for Foreign
Affairs as part of the Burgess Programme, headed for the French
Embassy in London by the Institut Français du Royaume Uni

Liberté • Égalité • Fraternité
RÉPUBLIQUE FRANÇAISE

This edition first published by Verso 1999
© Verso 1999
Translation © Gregory Elliott 1999
First published as *Écrits philosophiques et politiques. Tome II*
© Édition Stock/IMEC 1995
Paperback edition first published by Verso 2000

3 5 7 9 10 8 6 4

Verso
UK: 6 Meard Street, London W1F 0EG
US: 388 Atlantic Ave, Brooklyn, NY 11217
www.versobooks.com

Verso is the imprint of New Left Books

ISBN-13: 978-1-84467-675-0

British Library Cataloguing in Publication Data
A catalogue record for this book is available from the British Library

Library of Congress Cataloging-in-Publication Data
A catalog record for this book is available from the Library of Congress

Typeset by Hewer Text UK Ltd, Edinburgh
Printed by in the US

Contents

Editorial Note
François Matheron

Althusser's archives contain two different sets of texts derived from courses devoted to Machiavelli. The older of them dates back to 1962: it does not display the completion of the later material and is only partially written up. The second comprises two distinct versions of the text we are publishing under the title *Machiavelli and Us*, both numbered from page 1 to page 107.

The first version (bearing no title, but simply called 'Course') is an original typescript, revised with countless handwritten corrections and additions, which are difficult to date precisely. In a draft preface dated 1975 by Althusser, we read: 'These pages, which reproduce the notes for a course from 1965, repeated in 1972, could not claim, after so many others, to offer an "interpretation" of Machiavelli's œuvre.' However, since there is nothing to indicate that a course on Machiavelli was held in 1965, it is reasonable to assume that an error is involved, and that Althusser actually meant to refer to his 1962 course. If this is the case, then far from 'reproducing' his notes, he wrote a completely new text, very probably after 1968. Citing Maurice Merleau-Ponty's 'Note on Machiavelli', he refers to the reprint of this article in the collection *Éloge de la philosophie et autres essais*, published in 1965. But his own copy of the work, conserved in his library, in which he underlined precisely the passages quoted in this first version, contains the indication 'printed 20 December 1968'. And in a letter of 7 March 1972 to Henri Crétella, with whom he maintained a regular correspondence on Machiavelli and Gramsci, Althusser evokes his 1962 course, mislaid for the time being, and explains: 'All the documents and notes I ought to have assembled for this occasion have disappeared; I must have lent them to someone who didn't return them. . . . But this year, so ten years after, I have started all over again from scratch, and have done some lectures on Machiavelli: second offence.' In these circumstances, it may be assumed that this first version was composed in 1971–72.

The second version (the only one entitled *Machiavelli and Us* by Althusser) comprises two distinct units. The first thirteen pages are a new draft, rounded off with some handwritten revisions, of the opening of the preceding version (the first six pages in the form of a carbon copy, the remaining seven an original typescript). The rest of the text (pp. 14–107) is a photocopy of the first version, handwritten corrections included, itself rounded off with numerous additions and corrections. These handwritten revisions are of two sorts: some, primarily stylistic, are in black felt-tip; others, more substantive, in blue ballpoint. While it is extremely difficult to date this second version with precision, it is likely that many of the handwritten revisions were made in 1975–76, when Althusser wrote several draft prefaces. However, some addenda seem to date from much later: their content and written form make it reasonable to suppose that they are contemporaneous with 'Machiavelli, Philosopher', a handwritten text of nineteen pages drafted by Althusser on 11 July 1986.

It was impossible – and, it should be added, scarcely desirable – to indicate all the handwritten revisions. The following procedure has been adopted. Without signalling them, we have incorporated all Althusser's modifications to the first version of the text, opting to mention only the late corrections. We have adopted the same procedure for the new draft of the first thirteen pages of the work, in their entirety a belated revision of the text. In contrast, we have signalled the majority of the corrections made to the photocopied version; homogeneous, they mostly tend in the direction of the 'aleatory materialism' theorized by Louis Althusser in his last years. Difficult to date, these corrections are identified in the Notes where, like other editorial interpolations, they are indicated by '[E]'. When a more precise dating seemed possible, it has been given.

In the original French, all quotations from Machiavelli were taken from the Barincou edition of the *Œuvres complètes* published in the Bibliothèque de la Pléiade. For the English translation, on grounds of accessibility, separate editions of *The Prince* and the *Discourses on Livy* have been preferred to Gilbert's *The Chief Works and Others* (3 vols, Duke University Press, Durham, NC, 1965). All extracts, for whose use we are grateful to Cambridge University Press and Oxford University Press respectively, are from the following editions:

– *The Prince*, ed. Quentin Skinner and Russell Price, trans. Russell Price, Cambridge University Press, Cambridge 1988.

– *Discourses on Livy*, trans. Julia Conaway Bondanella and Peter Bondanella, Oxford University Press, Oxford and New York 1997.

To facilitate the intelligibility of Althusser's commentary, it has occasionally been necessary to modify the English rendition of Machiavelli, so that it conforms more closely to Barincou's French. Any such alterations are indicated in the standard fashion by the translator, who is grateful to Gillian Beaumont, Sebastian Budgen, Michael Sprinker, Lyn Thomas, and especially David Macey, for all their help. For the English edition of *Machiavelli and Us* we have appended 'Machiavelli's Solitude', the text of a lecture to the Association Française de Science Politique delivered by Althusser in 1977. It appears here in a slightly revised version of the translation by Ben Brewster originally published in *Economy and Society*, volume 17, number 4, November 1998 (pp. 168–79).

Introduction:
In the Mirror of Machiavelli
Gregory Elliott

'We do not publish our own drafts, that is, our own mistakes, but we do sometimes publish other people's,' Louis Althusser once observed of Marx's early writings.[1] Among his own posthumously published drafts, one, at least, is neither mistake nor out-take: 'Machiavel et nous'. Derived from a lecture course given in 1972, revised on and off up to the mid 1980s, and prepared for publication after his death in 1990, 'Machiavel et nous' eventually appeared in a 1995 collection of Althusser's philosophical and political writings.[2]

Four years earlier, commencing a remarkable paper on Althusser and Machiavelli, his former pupil Emmanuel Terray identified a paradox:

> The name of Machiavelli is rarely cited in Althusser's work. Apart from the 197[7] lecture on 'Machiavelli's Solitude' . . . , I can only find two citations of any importance. . . . A more meticulous and detailed examination . . . would turn up a few supplementary references. But it would not change the general impression that Machiavelli is explicitly present in Althusser's published works only occasionally and in a scattered way. Yet all who were taught orally by Althusser know it: this impression is misleading. It does not at all reflect the extreme importance that Althusser accorded to the thought of the Florentine Secretary, the historical role he recognized in him. In the presence of such silences, I always remember this verse by St.-John Perse: 'And the sun is unmentioned but his power is amongst us'. . . .[3]

In truth impeccably meticulous, Terray adduced the evidence available from two decades of Althusserian publications: assimilation of Machiavelli to the early-modern project of a *'moral or political physics'* in *Montesquieu: la politique et l'histoire* (1959); citation of Machiavelli the military strategist in 'Contradiction and Overdetermination' (1962); nomination of Machiavelli as originator of a 'theory of history' in *Éléments d'autocritique* (1974); invocation of Machiavelli's 'rule of Method . . . that one must think *in extremes'* in the *Soutenance* (1975); utilization of Machiavelli's critique of 'military expedients' against the 'fortress-like functioning' of the PCF in *Ce qui ne peut plus durer dans le parti communiste* (1978).[4] If this inventory of intermittent references corroborated Terray's 'general impression', Althusser's *Nachlass* vindicated not just the conviction of its deceptiveness, but his own intuitions as to the terrain of an encounter between the secretaries to the Florentine *signoria* and the Parisian *grande école* – an encounter about which there was little or nothing fortuitous.[5]

The encounter staged by Terray possessed textual licence in 'Machiavelli's Solitude', a lecture delivered to the Association Française de Science Politique in 1977 and initially published in German ten years later.[6] Included as an appendix to this volume, it elaborated on the 'rule of method' formulated in 1975. 'Machiavelli's Solitude' proved not to be an orphaned text. Where once the sun had largely gone unmentioned, in the late Althusser its power was summoned incessantly (what is probably his last philosophical composition, written in hospital in summer 1986, treated 'Machiavel philosophe'). The 1985 'traumabiography' *L'avenir dure longtemps*, released in 1992, contained a sprinkling of laudatory allusions to Machiavelli, alongside Spinoza, Epicurus and others, as so many directions on Althusser's 'royal road' to Marx.[7] The next year, chapters on Spinoza and Machiavelli withdrawn from *L'avenir* for incorporation into a projected work on 'La véritable tradition matérialiste' were published.[8] 'He is, without doubt, much more so than Marx, the author who has most fascinated me,' Althusser wrote of Machiavelli in the chapter allocated to Spinoza.[9] Why? According to another late work, 'Le courant souterrain du matérialisme de la rencontre' (1982), because Machiavelli pertained to *'a materialist tradition almost completely unrecognized in the history of philosophy'*, issuing from Epicurus:

a *materialism of the encounter*, hence of the aleatory and of contingency, which is completely opposed ... to the various registered materialisms, including the materialism commonly attributed to Marx, Engels and Lenin, which, like every materialism in the rationalist tradition, is a materialism of necessity and teleology, that is to say, a transformed and disguised form of idealism.[10]

Frequently admired as a secular theoretician of politics, as commonly decried as *the* cynical technician of power, Machiavelli had a quite different order of achievement to his credit: 'a philosophical theory of the encounter between fortune and *virtù*'.[11]

Althusser signalled his intention to develop these 'brief notes', stamped with the impress of the exasperated anti-finalism and nominalism of the aleatory turn of his last years.[12] Nothing with Althusser ever being simple, in fact he already had, in *Machiavelli and Us*, which as late as May 1986 he envisaged publishing in Spanish, but which saw the light of day only in 1995.

Whatever the detours of his road to Marx, Althusser's route to Machiavelli did not pass via the founders of historical materialism, even if Marx and Engels's denunciation of their opponents' 'Machiavellian policy' in the revolutionary conjuncture of 1848 is counterbalanced by incidental remarks thereafter.[13] Nor did it owe anything to the official culture of his party, where Machiavellianism was subjected to unstinting criticism by Georges Mounin in the late 1950s, in a work passed over in silence by Althusser.[14] Nor, once again, was his interest stimulated by French academic philosophy, in which (as he regretted when addressing the Société Française de Philosophie in 1968) Machiavelli was in good company as regards the neglect he had suffered until comparatively recently.[15] Notwithstanding Merleau-Ponty's 1949 'Note', which concluded that 'the problem of a real humanism that Machiavelli set was taken up again by Marx a hundred years ago', only with Augustin Renaudet's monograph of 1956 did the neglect begin to be seriously remedied.[16] Given the recognition bestowed upon Machiavelli by Montesquieu, Rousseau and others, Althusser was bound to have encountered him in his research for a projected thesis on 'politics and philosophy in the eighteenth century in France'.[17] But the royal road to a veritable Althusserian passion ran elsewhere.

In 1959 the PCF imprint Éditions Sociales issued a substantial selection from Gramsci's *Prison Notebooks*, including the material on the 'Modern Prince' which advanced an interpretation of Machiavelli exclusively focused on *The Prince* and cued by its hortatory closing chapter.[18] That Althusser had read Gramsci with attention and appreciation is evident from 'Contradiction and Overdetermination', drafted in the summer of 1962.[19] However, the *via italiana* was even more direct. On his own testimony, Althussser truly discovered Machiavelli the previous year in Italy, in the company of Franca Madonia, by whom he was captivated.[20] With the edition of the *Lettres à Franca*, published as this Introduction was being prepared, something of the extraordinary intensity of Althusser's engagement with his secret sharer from the summer of 1961 can now be gauged – an intensity prompting his correspondent to remonstrate that he had 'made a myth of [last] summer, . . . experienced it . . . as a veritable miracle, the house, . . . Italy, Machiavelli and Gramsci, and me'.[21]

By now sinking into an acute depression, on 11 January 1962 Althusser communicated to Franca his intention to attempt a course on Machiavelli, requesting her copy of the Feltrinelli edition of his *œuvre*. Subsequent letters of the 17th and 19th suggest that the first session took place on the 18th, and convey Althusser's dissatisfaction with its mediocrity. After a second session the following week, Althusser confided this revelation: 'under the guise of the supposed consciousness of Machiavelli, it was myself that I'd spoken about: a will to realism . . . and a "derealizing" situation'. On 1 February Althusser gave the final lecture of the series, devoted to Machiavelli's 'theoretical solitude'. A little over a fortnight later, he was hospitalized for three months.[22]

A long retrospective letter of 29 September 1962 pondered Althusser's elective 'affinity':

> It is no accident, I now think, that in the month-and-a-half preceding my collapse, I did this strange course on Machiavelli . . . the delirium of the course was nothing other than *my own delirium*. In particular, I remember the central theme I developed in it, namely that Machiavelli's fundamental problem was to *think* the conditions for the establishment of a 'new state' starting from a situation (that of Italy) in which conditions were at once wholly favourable . . . and wholly

unfavourable . . . so that Machiavelli's central problem from a *theoretical* viewpoint could be summed up in the question of the *beginning, starting from nothing, of an absolutely indispensable and necessary* new state. I'm not inventing anything, I'm not fabricating this thought, Franca. But in elaborating this theoretical problem and its implications, in expounding the theoretical consequences (in particular, the theory of fortune and *virtù*), I had the hallucinatory sense (of an irresistible force) . . . of elaborating nothing other than *my own delirium*. . . . The question I dealt with: how *to begin from nothing* . . . was *mine*!

Confident that he had now 'personally resolved Machiavelli's problem', Althusser reckoned he could dispense with 'the miraculous mirror of Machiavelli'.[23]

He had not resolved the problem (soon enough he was reverting to it with Franca).[24] And he never broke his identification with the author of *The Prince* – if not *speculum principii*, then mirror for a philosopher obsessed with the solitude of the (re)founding moment. Althusser recognized himself in the solitude stipulated by Book 1, Chapter 9 of the *Discourses*, glossed as *'every absolute beginning requires the absolute solitude of the reformer or founder'*. Machiavelli's 'contradictory demand' – a foundation or reformation at once indispensable and yet unrealizable – reflected, *mutatis mutandis*, Althusser's own relationship to historical Communism.[25]

Only partially written up, the 1962 course was manifestly far from delirious. Endorsing the republican estimates of Machiavelli by Spinoza and Rousseau, it rejected his execration in the black legend of Machiavellianism. More importantly, it introduced a Gramscian grid, following the *Prison Notebooks* in foregrounding the last chapter of *The Prince*, with its summons 'to liberate Italy from the barbarian yoke', and construing Machiavelli as the precocious, unseasonable thinker of Italian unity. As Antonio Negri has noted, this was a rendition of Machiavelli 'situated in the tradition of Romanticism and the thought of the Italian Risorgimento, from Foscolo to De Sanctis, right up to Della Volpe'.[26] Wherein consisted his 'singularity' for Althusser in 1962?

Machiavelli . . . formulates the problem neglected by classical thought: the problem of the appearance of absolute monarchy. . . . He finds himself confronting a problem which is posed him by foreign countries ... but which he poses in connection with Italy, that is to say, a country not in a condition to resolve it or even pose it in real terms. This is why Machiavelli finds himself in the privileged situation of being the imaginary witness of a real event, or the real witness of an imaginary event. His whole theory is summed up in the thought of this event, and his whole theory, all its distinctive concepts, are only the impotent thought of this event, of the advent of this event. This is why, at the level of concepts, it is so contradictory, and in fact, when all is said and done, is no sooner constructed than it disintegrates.[27]

Although irreducible to mere empiricism, Machiavelli's break with the classical political tradition had been retarded by the underdeveloped historical reality of the *Cinquecento*, rendering his thought 'a consciousness without science but also without theory'.[28]

Althusser's attribution of an unconsummated rupture to Machiavelli was to be taken up by his pupil François Regnault, in the one text (to my knowledge) directly inspired by the 1962 course. Arguing that Machiavelli 'reasons *by* examples', Regnault credited him with the 'materialism in history' over which Althusser was to enthuse in *Machiavelli and Us*.[29]

The immediate reasons for Althusser's recidivism a decade after his first foray into Machiavelli are not apparent; its occasion is. Althusser's work started life as a course for candidates of the philosophy *agrégation* at the École normale supérieure in January–February 1972, and was followed by lectures on Rousseau's *Discourse on the Origin of Inequality* in which (according to one who attended them) 'Althusser laid bare the structure of that difficult text in a masterly fashion'.[30] Around 1975–76 Althusser significantly modified his course – especially the introduction – gave it its present title, and penned a preface. Having summarized its conclusions in the lecture on 'Machiavelli's Solitude' in 1977, Althusser returned to *Machiavelli and Us* during his final decade, revising references to the 'dialectic' and 'dialectical materialism' by a systematic induction of the discourse of 'aleatory materialism'.[31]

Whether *Machiavelli and Us* holds more of a mirror up to its author than to his subject will be left to readers to decide for themselves. In his massive *Le Travail de l'œuvre: Machiavel*, published the autumn after Althusser's 1972 course, Claude Lefort

reproved the tendency of commentators to advertise both Machiavelli's 'enigma' and their claim to have solved it: 'not one . . .
is content to offer .a new perspective'.[32] Lavishing praise on
Lefort in his foreword, Althusser renounced any such ambition,
precisely contenting himself with 'another perspective' on an
'enigma' which had led Croce to venture that the Machiavelli
question would never be 'settled'.

    If Althusser's alternative perspective and references are unset-
tling to an Anglophone audience familiar with the modern
scholarship encapsulated in Quentin Skinner's *Machiavelli*, it is
nevertheless worth registering a certain commonality of purpose.
Skinner's intellectual biography maintains that 'in order to
understand Machiavelli's doctrines, we need to begin by recov-
ering the problems he evidently saw himself confronting'.[33] For
Skinner, naturally, such contextualization could not bypass the
philological resource of the original Italian texts, whereas Althusser largely (if not exclusively) relies upon Barincou's Pléiade
edition.[34] Even so, he too was intent upon a recovery of Machiavelli's problems, the better to displace traditional controversies
over the Florentine diplomat (e.g. whether he was the founder
of positive 'political science'), and display him instead as what
(transposing Negri's classification of Spinoza) we might call 'the
savage anomaly'. For Althusser, Machiavelli does not merely
criticize the Renaissance humanism rooted in classical antiquity
(as when he silently contradicts Book I of Cicero's *Moral Obliga-
tion* on force and fraud as 'unworthy of man'). In pursuit of *la
verità effettuale della cosa*, Machiavelli unequivocally repudiates it,
together with 'the entire tradition of Christian theology and all
the political theories of antiquity' (pp. 7–8). The upshot is 'Machiavelli's solitude', stranded as he is between classical and Christian traditions, on the one hand, and the modern tradition of
natural law theory, on the other.[35]

    As Timothy O'Hagan has remarked: '[I]f Althusser's Machia-
velli is solitary, his reading of Machiavelli is not.'[36] Anticipated
by Hegel in 1802, elaborated by De Sanctis in 1870, and adopted
by Gramsci in the 1930s, according to it the overriding 'problem'
posed to and by Machiavelli is 'the constitution of Italian
national unity' (p. 53). But while he shares this sense of the
Machiavellian problematic, and the correlative conception of *The
Prince* as a 'revolutionary utopian manifesto', Althusser reinte-

grates the *Discourses*, with their reasoning by comparisons, into it. Quite the reverse of the inconsistency alleged by commentators between the monarchistic *Prince* and the republican *Discourses*, Machiavelli's 'theoretical utopia' discloses a 'profound unity' in which a monarchy is to the foundation, as a republic is to the duration, of one and the same object: a national-popular state (pp. 65–6).

The main innovation of the Althusserian reading lies elsewhere. He fixes upon Machiavelli's *dispositif théorique*, and its effects on 'the modality of [his] object', as the key to his philosophical importance. The peculiarity of this *dispositif* – a term notoriously difficult to render in English, but here translated 'dispositive' on the advice of David Macey – is to state a series of general theses on history which are literally contradictory, yet organized in such a way as to generate concepts not deducible from them, for the purpose of theorizing an '*"object" which is in fact a determinate objective*' (p. 42). Machiavelli's 'endeavour to think the conditions of possibility of an impossible task, to think the unthinkable' induces 'a strange *vacillation* in the traditional philosophical status of [his] theoretical propositions: as if they were undermined by another instance than the one that produces them – the instance of political practice' (pp. 52, 20). Inscribing in itself the place of the political practice which alone can determine the identity of 'a New Prince in a New Principality', Machiavelli's theory of the conjuncture inhabits the space of the putatively universal – the abstract-theoretical – to think the irreducibly singular – the concrete-historical case of sixteenth-century Italy. If 'the first theorist of the conjuncture' (p. 18) can specify the preconditions for a fruitful 'encounter' between *virtù* (or the political agency of the Prince) and fortune (or the contingency of the real), his grasp of the necessity of contingency precludes any prediction of what is, by definition, aleatory.

The encounter staged *par personne interposée* in Terray's essay had thus well and truly taken place, on an identical terrain and to similar effect: what Negri has dubbed 'a materialism of singularity', imputed to the trio of Machiavelli, Spinoza and Marx, but perfected in the *œuvre* of the first, whose profound historical and political realism was upheld.[37] Already discernible in the recurrent tension in the Althusser of the 1960s between the analyst of singular conjunctures and the theoretician of invariant structures, this 'materialism' undergoes magnification in the mirror of Machiavelli after 1980. In a letter sent to Franca Madonia while he was at work on *Reading Capital*, Althusser had critically adjudged Gramsci 'the Machiavelli of modern times', asserting that 'he reads Lenin through Machiavelli, just as he reads Machiavelli through Lenin'.[38] With due alteration of detail, does the last Althusser invite an altogether dissimilar verdict?

A final unsettled question concerns Althusser's title. In the event, it had been employed before, by Louis de Villefosse, whose *Machiavel et nous* (1937) identified the 'armed prophets' and practitioners of *Realpolitik* – Mussolini, Hitler and Stalin – as the makers of twentieth-century history.[39] But to whom is Althusser's essay addressed? Has 'the addressee disappear[ed] with the address', as Althusser argued occurs if *The Prince* is reduced to 'recipes of tyranny and villainy' (p. 31)? After all – *pace* Lacan – '*it happens that a letter does not arrive at its destination.*'[40] No response will be hazarded here. In reaction to those who depict Machiavelli as 'diabolical', Skinner closes by affirming that '[t]he business of the historian . . . is surely to serve as a recording angel, not a hanging judge'.[41] It is for recipients of this philosophico-political letter from afar to condemn or commend it. An intellectual historian is content to record belated delivery.

Notes

1. Appendix to 'Réponse à une critique' (1963), in Althusser, *Écrits philosophiques et politiques. Tome II*, ed. and intro. François Matheron, Éditions Stock/IMEC, Paris 1995, p. 385.
2. *Écrits philosophiques et politiques. Tome II*, pp. 39–168.
3. Emmanuel Terray, 'An Encounter: Althusser and Machiavelli', trans. Antonio Callari and David F. Ruccio, in Callari and Ruccio, eds, *Postmodern Materialism and the Future of Marxist Theory: Essays in the Althusserian Tradition*, University Press of New England, Hanover and London 1996, pp. 257–77 (here pp. 257–8; trans. modified). Given at a 1991 colloquium on Althusser, Terray's paper was first published in French in 1993.
4. See *Politics and History: Montesquieu, Rousseau, Hegel and Marx*, trans. Ben Brewster, New Left Books, London 1972, pp. 17, 24; *For Marx*, trans. Ben Brewster, Allen Lane, London 1969, p. 94; *Essays in Self-Criticism*, trans. Grahame Lock, New Left Books, London 1976, p. 136; *Philosophy and the Spontaneous Philosophy of the Scientists & Other Essays*, trans. Ben Brewster *et al.*, Verso, London and New York 1990, pp. 206, 209; 'What Must Change in the French Communist Party', trans. Patrick Camiller, *New Left Review* 109, May/June 1978, p. 44. The only other significant references I have traced in material released during Althusser's lifetime occur in texts originally pub-

lished in languages other than French. See 'The Transformation of Philosophy' (1976), issued in Spanish but not in French until 1994, where Machiavelli is credited with the inauguration of 'political theory' and conjoined with Epicurus as a subject for further research (*Philosophy and the Spontaneous Philosophy of the Scientists & Other Essays*, pp. 257, 261); and 'On Marx and Freud' (1976), published in German in 1977 but in French only in 1993, where Machiavelli's formula in the 'Dedicatory Letter' of *The Prince* is applied to the vantage-point of the proletariat in a knowledge of capitalism (Althusser, *Writings on Psychoanalysis: Freud and Lacan*, trans. Jeffrey Mehlman, Columbia University Press, New York 1996, pp. 111–12).

5. See Terray's conclusion to 'An Encounter: Althusser and Machiavelli', p. 276.
6. Translated from a copy of the French typescript by Ben Brewster, 'Machiavelli's Solitude' appeared in *Economy and Society*, vol. 17, no. 4, November 1988, pp. 468–79, with an excellent introduction by Timothy O'Hagan, pp. 461–7. A somewhat shorter French version was subsequently published in *Futur antérieur*, no. 1, Spring 1990, pp. 26–40. It is now reprinted in Althusser, *Solitude de Machiavel et autres textes*, ed. Yves Sintomer, Presses Universitaires de France, Paris 1998, pp. 311–24.
7. See *The Future Lasts a Long Time and The Facts*, trans. Richard Veasey, Chatto & Windus, London 1993, pp. 215–16; see also pp. 103–4, 211, 220, 241–2.
8. 'L'unique tradition matérialiste', *Lignes*, no. 18, January 1993, pp. 72–119; reprinted in the second edition of *L'avenir dure longtemps, suivi de Les Faits*, ed. Olivier Corpet and Yann Moulier Boutang, Le Livre de Poche, Paris 1994, pp. 467–507. The Spinoza chapter has now been translated by Ted Stolze in Warren Montag and Ted Stolze, eds, *The New Spinoza*, University of Minnesota Press, Minneapolis and London 1997, pp. 3–18.
9. *The New Spinoza*, p. 13.
10. 'Le courant souterrain du matérialisme de la rencontre', in Althusser, *Écrits philosophiques et politiques. Tome I*, ed. and introd. François Matheron, Éditions Stock/IMEC, Paris 1994, pp. 539–79 (here pp. 539–40). See also 'Philosophie et marxisme – Entretiens avec Fernanda Navarro (1984–87)', in Althusser, *Sur la philosophie*, ed. Olivier Corpet, Éditions Gallimard, Paris 1994, pp. 13–79 (esp. pp. 29–48). In an excised passage of the original French typescript of 'Solitude de Machiavel' (p. 16), Althusser had already attributed a philosophical 'materialism derived from Epicurus' to Machiavelli.
11. *Écrits philosophiques et politiques. Tome I*, p. 545. For Althusser's discussion of Machiavelli, see pp. 543–8.
12. Ibid., p. 548.
13. Compare, for example, Marx and Engels, *Selected Correspondence*, Progress Publishers, Moscow 1975, p. 91 (Marx's letter of 25 September 1857, praising the *History of Florence* as a 'masterpiece'), with *Collected Works*, vol. 7, Lawrence & Wishart, London 1979, p. 212 (where a 'Machiavellian policy' seeking 'to paralyse democratic energies' is denounced). See also Engels, *Dialectics of Nature*, Progress Publishers, Moscow 1954, p. 21, where Machiavelli is cited as 'the first notable military author of modern times'.
14. Georges Mounin, *Machiavel*, Club français du livre, Paris 1958. For differing estimates, compare Claude Lefort, *Le Travail de l'œuvre: Machiavel*, Éditions Gallimard, Paris 1972, pp. 133–47, with Perry Anderson, *Lineages of the Absolutist State*, New Left Books, London 1974, p. 168 n. 51. Both Mounin and Lefort discuss a significant episode in the strained relations between Marxism and Machiavellianism: Prosecutor-General Vyshinsky's use of Kamenev's 1934 Preface to Machiavelli against its author, at the first of the Moscow trials in 1936. For the text in question, see Lev Kamenev, 'Preface to

Machiavelli', *New Left Review* 15, May/June 1962, pp. 39–42, preceded by Chimen Abramsky, 'Kamenev's Last Essay', pp. 34–8.

15. See 'Lenin and Philosophy' (1968), in *Philosophy and the Spontaneous Philosophy of the Scientists & Other Essays*, p. 173.

16. Maurice Merleau-Ponty, 'A Note on Machiavelli', in Merleau-Ponty, *Signs*, trans. Richard C. McCleary, Northwestern University Press, Evanston, IL 1964, pp. 211–23 (here p. 222); Augustin Renaudet, *Machiavel*, Éditions Gallimard, Paris 1956. Both authors are cited by Althusser in *Machiavelli and Us*. According to François Matheron, '[a] heavily annotated copy of Renaudet's work was found in Althusser's library': p. 109 n. 51 below.

17. 'Is it Simple to be a Marxist in Philosophy?', in *Philosophy and the Spontaneous Philosophy of the Scientists & Other Essays*, p. 205.

18. Antonio Gramsci, *Selections from the Prison Notebooks*, ed. and trans. Quintin Hoare and Geoffrey Nowell Smith, Lawrence & Wishart, London 1971, pp. 125–43. For a contemporary commentary, see Benedetto Fontana, *Hegemony and Power: On the Relation between Gramsci and Machiavelli*, University of Minnesota Press, Minneapolis and London 1993.

19. See *For Marx*, pp. 105–6 n. 23; 114 and n. 29.

20. See *L'avenir dure longtemps*, p. 481 (unaccountably, the year is given as 1964 in *The New Spinoza*, p. 13).

21. Franca Madonia, letter of 2 February 1962, in Althusser, *Lettres à Franca (1961–1973)*, ed. François Matheron and Yann Moulier Boutang, Éditions Stock/IMEC, Paris 1998, p. 165. (I am grateful to Messieurs Matheron and Moulier Boutang for supplying me with a copy of this superb volume, making it possible to take it into account here.)

22. For this sequence of letters, see ibid., pp. 151, 155–6, 162–3, 169.

23. Ibid., pp. 223–4, 226.

24. See Althusser's letter of 26 April 1963, in ibid., p. 412.

25. See below, pp. 64, 51–2 and François Matheron's penetrating commentary in 'Louis Althusser ou l'impure pureté du concept', *Actuel Marx*, forthcoming. (I am grateful to the author for furnishing me with a copy of this text.)

26. Antonio Negri, 'Machiavel selon Althusser', in Gabriel Albiac *et al.*, *Lire Althusser aujourd'hui*, *Futur antérieur*/L'Harmattan, Paris 1997, pp. 139–57 (here p. 142). On the 1962 course, see pp. 140–44, on which I have drawn above.

27. Quoted by François Matheron in his presentation of *Écrits philosophiques et politiques. Tome II*, pp. 11–12.

28. Quoted in Negri, 'Machiavel selon Althusser', p. 143.

29. François Regnault, 'La pensée du prince', *Cahiers pour l'analyse*, no. 6, *La Politique des philosophes*, January/February 1967, pp. 23–52 (here pp. 34, 48 n. 1). Althusser is acknowledged at p. 23 n. 1.

30. See O'Hagan, '"Machiavelli's Solitude": An Introduction', pp. 462–3, 466 n. 8.

31. See 'Editorial Note' above, pp. vii–viii; and Negri, 'Machiavel selon Althusser', pp. 144 ff.

32. Lefort, *Le Travail de l'œuvre*, pp. 9, 35.

33. Quentin Skinner, *Machiavelli*, Oxford University Press, Oxford 1981, pp. 1–2. Skinner's text has been translated into French (Éditions Gallimard, Paris 1989) by Michel Plon, an ex-Althusserian who contributed a text on Machiavelli to an Althusser obituary issue of the journal *M*: see 'Machiavel, de la politique comme un impossible', *M: Mensuel, marxisme, mouvement*, no. 43, January 1991, pp. 25–7.

34. In this connection, note Lefort's comments on the need, especially in the case of the *Discourses*, 'to try to restore in French the precise intention, which is

too often distorted by a concern for elegance or the fear of repeating terms': *Le Travail de l'œuvre*, p. 313 n.

35. O'Hagan ('"Machiavelli's Solitude": An Introduction', p. 466 n. 4) notes the 'similar view of Machiavelli's "originality"' taken by Isaiah Berlin in his famous essay of 1953; see 'The Originality of Machiavelli', in Berlin, *Against the Current: Essays in the History of Ideas*, ed. Henry Hardy, Hogarth Press, London 1980, pp. 25–79, esp. pp. 36 ff.

36. O'Hagan, '"Machiavelli's Solitude": An Introduction', p. 462.

37. Negri, 'Machiavel selon Althusser', p. 140. For a critical account of Machiavelli's 'unseeing empiricism' and consequent 'voluntarism', see Anderson, *Lineages of the Absolutist State*, pp. 163–9.

38. Letter of 2 July 1965, in *Lettres à Franca*, p. 624. Althusser would have been aware of Croce's description of Marx as 'a Machiavelli of the labour movement' in *Historical Materialism and the Economics of Karl Marx*.

39. See Lefort, *Le Travail de l'œuvre*, p. 126 and n. 2. Machiavelli's counterposition of 'armed' to 'unarmed' prophets was, of course, to be adopted by Isaac Deutscher for his magnificent biography of Trotsky.

40. 'The Discovery of Dr Freud' (1976), in Althusser, *Writings on Psychoanalysis: Freud and Lacan*, p. 92.

41. Skinner, *Machiavelli*, p. 88, specifically referring to Leo Strauss, *Thoughts on Machiavelli*, University of Washington Press, Seattle and London 1969. The text of lectures given in 1953, Strauss's work, originally published in 1958, portrays Machiavelli as a 'teacher of evil' and 'Machiavellianism' as the antithesis of 'Americanism'.

Machiavelli and Us

Foreword

Before launching into the risky venture of this essay,[1] I should like to pay a well-deserved homage to a thesis on Machiavelli published three or four years ago: Claude Lefort's *Le Travail de l'œuvre*.[2] For I know of no analysis as acute and intelligent of an author who, from the time he wrote, has always perplexed his readers. And although Lefort denies offering an 'interpretation' of them, I am not aware of any commentary on *The Prince* and the *Discourses on Livy* that goes so far in understanding Machiavelli's cast of mind and turn of phrase – and never mind the transcendental philosophy *à la* Merleau-Ponty in which it is arbitrarily wrapped. Should it ever be discovered – as the outcome of an investigation of unprecedented meticulousness – for whom Machiavelli wrote, we owe it, in the first instance, to Lefort.

Consequently, I have no intention of repeating, even remotely, something that has already been done so well, or of summarizing it. I should like to offer another perspective on Machiavelli: the sense shared by all his immediate readers, for whom he also wrote, of not sharing his secrets. The sense we share too, as if, by a miracle that requires elucidation, we were the contemporaries of his first anonymous readers.

Here we are: neither predisposed to him nor prejudiced against him, we read Machiavelli and, as De Sanctis put it so well, 'he takes us by surprise, and leaves us pensive'.[3] Pensive. As if a first thought, which we thought we had grasped on a first reading, stayed in the mind in the form of unexpected thoughts; as if the sentences, associated in our memory, combined in new formations yielding novel meanings; as if, from one chapter to the next, like the landscapes of this great walker, new perspectives were disclosed to us: all the more gripping because they had not been made out sooner.

The word has been let slip: gripping. Machiavelli grips us. But if by chance we want to grasp him, he evades us: he is elusive.

I wished to reflect on this enigma, this strangeness, this 'strange familiarity' of which Freud once spoke, precisely in connection with works of art. On this paradox. On this enduring actuality despite the passage of centuries, as if from his province, home to men and beasts, Machiavelli had come down among us and spoken to us since time immemorial.

I venture these associations. If they are reckoned too personal, no matter, since they still refer to him. If they have the good fortune to interest a few people who, on issues over which so many adversaries had clashed, recognize in his words the real nature of the battle they were waging, then so much the better. But it is still him we have to thank. And if – as, indeed, chance may have it – I overstep his field of thought, let us say that he opened up this space, among others, to us.

L. A.
September 1976

Theory and Political Practice

In Book III of *The Art of War* (a dialogue), Fabrizio, who represents Machiavelli's viewpoint, is discussing the new artillery weapon with Luigi. The debate is about whether cannon can be used within the ranks of troops on the march. And Fabrizio replies: 'You must know that . . . cannon, especially those on carriages, cannot be kept within the troops, *because when they are moving they face in the opposite direction to that in which they fire.*'[1]

I would not want to make too much of this quip. But it might serve – after its fashion, and in allegorical mode – to sum up the impression of a philosophical reader confronted with Machiavelli: more specifically, a philosophical reader who wishes to enrol Machiavelli *in his own ranks.* He will rapidly have come to realize that Machiavelli 'marches in the opposite direction to that in which he fires', or fires in the opposite direction from that in which one wishes to make him march; or, even worse, that if he certainly does not fire in the line of the march, we do not even know where he is firing: he always fires elsewhere.

This remark is to signal the extreme difficulty of reflecting on Machiavelli philosophically. It would be too easy to respond that he dealt only with politics and history, and is not a philosopher, for his discourse exceeds its apparent object with a singular meaning that intrigues the philosopher. It would be too hasty to suggest that Machiavelli is the antiphilosopher, philosophy's other. For which other exactly? Were it obliged to say, philosophy would be highly embarrassed. Of ten testimonies to the 'enigma' of Machiavelli, I shall retain only that of Merleau-Ponty, who indicates this embarrassment with his opening words, 'How could he have been understood?', later replying: 'The reason why Machiavelli is not understood . . .'.[2] I set aside Merleau-Ponty's response (Machiavelli combines contingency in the world and consciousness in man), but accept his question. The fact that it could still have been posed in 1949 in Florence, at a conference on humanism and political science, signifies that it had not been answered; that it was – and remains – unavoidable; and hence that Machiavelli confronts philosophy with a singular, and singularly difficult, question: that of his comprehension.

Let us try to define this difficulty. I would say that what strikes every reader of Machiavelli's texts is their triple character: they are gripping, but elusive, and thus strange.

Gripping: all the great classical authors celebrated the startling, astounding character of Machiavelli – from Spinoza, in veiled terms in paragraph two of the *Political Treatise*, to Gramsci, via Montesquieu, Hegel, Marx, and various others. The style of *The Prince*, that brilliant opuscule keen as a blade, is invoked. But it is the thought that stands out sharply, disconcerts, and captivates.

At the end of his life, Croce himself declared that the vexed question of Machiavelli would 'never be settled'.[3]

To what should we attribute this capacity to startle? Machiavelli himself offers an answer. On several occasions in *The Prince* and the *Discourses*, he writes that what especially surprises men is something new: the never previously seen. Let us range beyond an explanation which might be characterized as 'psychological', and which apparently simply recycles some variations of classical philosophy on amazement. Machiavelli is the theorist of something new solely because he is the theorist of beginnings (we shall see why and how) – of *the* beginning. Novelty can only repose on the surface of things; it can only affect an aspect of things, and fades with the moment that induced it. In contrast, the beginning is, so to speak, rooted in the essence of a thing, since it is the beginning of *this* thing. It affects all its determinations, and does not fade with the moment, but *endures* with the thing itself. If one considers the thing which begins, and is novel because it begins, before it there was something else, but nothing of it. The novelty of the beginning thus grips us for two reasons: because of the contrast between the after and the before, the new and the old; and because of their opposition and their impact, their rupture.

Let us apply Machiavelli to Machiavelli, and we shall understand that if he is gripping, it is not simply because he is new, but because he represents a *beginning*. He himself writes, on the very first page of the *Discourses*: 'Although the envious nature of men has always made it no less perilous to discover new methods and institutions than to search for unknown lands and seas, ... nevertheless ... I have resolved to enter upon a path still untrodden, ... though it may bring me distress and difficulty.'[4] In *The Prince* he announces the 'originality' of his work and the 'importance' of its subject matter.[5]

Discovery, an untrodden path, unknown lands and seas: new because unknown, unprecedented. Machiavelli declares himself thus. What begins with him? A 'true understanding' of history, of rulers, of the art of governing and making war – in short, everything traditionally designated as the foundation of a positive science, the science of politics. I shelve the question of whether these terms (positive science of politics) are correct. At all events, they register a beginning that is a foundation – the beginning of a 'thing' (this science) that persists down to the present – and, correlatively, a contrast and rupture.

Machiavelli himself supplies the formula that sanctions this beginning and this rupture. It is famous: *'mi è parso più conveniente andare dietro alla verità effettuale della cosa, che all'immaginazione di essa'* ('it seems to me better to represent things as they are in actual truth, rather than as they are imagined').[6] This formula counterposes the 'actual truth', hence objective knowledge, of things to imaginary, subjective representation. Objective knowledge of the 'thing' with which he deals – politics (i.e. political practice) – this is Machiavelli's innovation; and it contrasts sharply with what prevailed previously: an imaginary representation of politics, an ideology of politics. Similarly, when he refers to a 'true understanding' of history, he clearly stands out against its imaginary representation. Through his silences even more than his words, we may infer which discourses Machiavelli condemns definitively: not only the *edifying* religious, moral or aesthetic discourses of the court humanists, and even radical humanists; not only the revolutionary sermons of a Savonarola; but also the entire tradition of Christian theology and all the political theories of antiquity. How can we fail to notice that with the exception of Aristotle, cited once in passing,[7] Machiavelli never invokes the great political texts of Plato, Aristotle, the Epicureans, the Stoics, Cicero? He who admired antiquity so much, he whose thought was nurtured on examples drawn from the history of Athens, Sparta and Rome, never explained himself on this score except by silence. But at a time when no one discussed politics except in the language of Aristotle, Cicero and Christianity, this silence stood for a declaration of rupture. It was enough for Machiavelli to speak differently to denounce the imaginary character of the reigning ideology in political matters.

It is evident that Machiavelli considered himself the founder of a theory without any precedent, and that between the reigning imaginary representations of history and politics and his knowledge of the 'actual truth of the thing' there is an abyss, the emptiness of a distance taken, that cannot but startle. Indeed, from his viewpoint – that of the actual truth of the thing – he discovers (as Spinoza will later say: *verum index sui et falsi*) both the actual truth of the thing *and* the imaginary character of the representations inherited from antiquity and Christianity. 'It is', he writes, 'an evil not to call evil an evil.' The evil that harms rulers and peoples is imaginary representations. Machiavelli gives it a name – imagination – and moves on. He speaks the truth, which indicates the false, so as to condemn falsity and pave the way for truth. That he is original, that he is a founder, that he conquered his thought against the whole dominant ideology – this is what already makes Machiavelli gripping for us.

However, Machiavelli holds a greater surprise than this in store. For how are we to understand that this beginning has lasted down to the present, and still endures for us? What Machiavelli did has not remained in its initial state. History has transformed it. Spinoza, Montesquieu and Marx (to cite only them), who praise him, have either inflected, or continued, or utterly transformed his work. Not only are Machiavelli's writings no longer novel for us, they are outmoded, even outdated. We have known novelties and beginnings in politics other than *The Prince* and the *Discourses*. Yet these texts are not any the less gripping, but remain so. There must be some reason other than the surprise [*surprise*] of a theoretical discovery: a purchase [*prise*] on politics, on its *practice*.

To make this effect felt, I shall take two well-known examples: Hegel and Gramsci.

In his 1802 essay 'On the German Constitution',[8] Hegel offers an emotive eulogy of Machiavelli, whose genius he celebrates against all the moralizing critics who have belaboured him. He celebrates him, not for having preferred the actual truth of the thing to its imagination, but for another reason. Obviously, Hegel's philosophy must be taken into consideration, since Hegel cannot reflect on Machiavelli without subjecting him to the development of the concept in the objective Spirit's self-realization. As such, Machiavelli is presented as the man of the state, the man of the concept of the state – or, more precisely, as the man who possesses the 'instinct of the state', and who is thus, rather than the man of the state, precisely a statesman, *Staatsmann*. A strange statesman, this man who never ruled or governed anything! All the same, Hegelian philosophy relates Machiavelli to history and politics in this way. And it is on this account that he interests Hegel, for he 'speaks' to him historically and politically.

Machiavelli does not speak to Hegel in the past tense, as the founder, already old, of a theory of politics. He 'speaks' to him in the present and, quite specifically, of the German political situation. In his text, with its famous opening sentence: '*Deutschland ist kein Staat mehr*' ('Germany is a state no longer'), Hegel adopts the accents of Machiavelli speaking of Italy. The same dismemberment, same dispersion, same particularisms, same impotence, same disarray, same political 'misery'. Only one solution: the constitution of a state, in this country suffering from its absence. For Hegel, Machiavelli's actuality is to have had the audacity to pose and treat the political (and, in Hegel's view, philosophical) problem of the constitution of a state in a split, divided country condemned to the assaults of foreign states. Of course, Hegel has in mind the Idea of the state, bolstered by his entire philosophy of the Idea, whereas Machiavelli possesses only the 'instinct' of the state. But if the peculiarity of Hegel's philosophy is to find itself at home – *bei sich* – in every object and theorist, even one so strange as Machiavelli; if Hegel is political solely in the element of speculative philosophy, something nevertheless transpires in this encounter that pertains not simply to Hegelian philosophy but to a certain manner of thinking, arguing and talking politics that touched Hegel in Machiavelli. Let us say: what is 'in play' is the *formulation of a political problem* that confronted Germany at the very beginning of the nineteenth century, in terms formally analogous to those defined for sixteenth-century Italy by Machiavelli. Can we be more precise? A certain way of thinking about politics, not for its own sake, but in the shape of the formulation of a problem and the definition of a historical task – this is what surprises Hegel, and breaks open the empire of his own philosophical consciousness.

The same is true of Gramsci; yet there is a difference.[9] A difference, because Gramsci naturally ridicules the Idea of the state, as well as the rational necessity of elevating a people without a state to the historical and philosophical dignity of the state. He goes *'dietro alla verità effettuale della cosa'*, and calls things by their name. The state that Machiavelli expects from the Prince, for the unification of Italy under an absolute monarch, is not the state in general (corresponding 'to its concept') but a historically determinate type of state, required by the conditions and exigencies of nascent capitalism: a *national* state. But when Gramsci wrote the pages evincing his passion for Machiavelli in his prison cell, Italy had already achieved its unity sixty years before. Gramsci discovers the means of understanding the political project to which Machiavelli devoted all his efforts in the intervening years, the long and painful birth of the Italian nation-state. And since Italian unity is still not actually – that is to say, socially – realized – if only because of the existence of the southern question – we may suppose that Machiavelli 'speaks' to Gramsci, if in large part historically and retrospectively, for the same reasons that he 'spoke' to Hegel: because he had the audacity to state the *'verità effettuale della cosa'*, to pose the *political* problem of the constitution (to be accomplished) of Italian unity.

However, something else transpires between Machiavelli and Gramsci. If Machiavelli speaks to Gramsci, it is not in the past tense, but in the present: better still, in the future.

For convenience's sake, it might be said that the 'theoretical' surprise is a surprise from the past. Hegel's 'political' surprise is the surprise of the present; Gramsci's, that of the future.

Gramsci's master theme – perhaps not well spotted by Lefort – is the following. Machiavelli formulated, in masterly fashion, the political question of Italian unity – that is to say, the political problem of the Italian nation's constitution by means of a national state. More precisely, Machiavelli grasped that as soon as the history of the initial development of the mercantile and capitalist bourgeoisie posed the problem of the constitution and definition of nations in specific geographical, linguistic and cultural zones, it imposed the solution: a nation can be constituted only by means of a state – a national state.

What need does the existence – and hence constitution – of nations answer? Above all, the need for the creation of material – and thus social – market zones where the industrial and commercial activity of the nascent bourgeoisie can be conducted and developed in a process of expanded reproduction. The constitution of these nations is, of course, effected in and through determinate forms of class struggle (Machiavelli knows it), pitting the elements of the new, growing mode of production against the dominant forms of the feudal mode of production. Class struggle is at the heart of the constitution of nations: the nation represents the form of existence indispensable to the implantation of the capitalist mode of production, in its struggle against the forms of the feudal mode of production.

But the need for the existence and constitution of a nation is one thing; the factual and relatively aleatory conditions of its realization are quite another. While the need to constitute the nation ultimately corresponds to the creation of a sufficiently large market for the nascent bourgeoisie, the nation cannot be constituted by decree. It is the stake of a class struggle. But the outcome of this struggle – whose objective is not the conquest of an already existing form, but the reality of a form that does not as yet exist – depends upon the arrangement of the existing elements. To put it another way, the possibilities and limits of the nation's realization depend upon a whole series of factors – not only economic, but also pre-existing geographical, historical, linguistic and cultural factors – which in some sense prestructure the aleatory space in which the nation will be able to take shape. Thus, Machiavelli notes that it is easy to annex – that is to say, unify under the same political authority – peoples who share the same customs and language, but not others.[10] Obviously, the constitution of a nation also (and sometimes in a determinate manner) depends upon the relations of force between the various nations in the process of being constituted. Machiavelli's Italy, subject to the incessant invasions of French and Spanish troops, is the negative proof.

But a nation is not constituted spontaneously. The pre-existing elements are not unified into a nation of their own accord. An instrument is required to forge its unity, assemble its real or potential elements, defend the unity that has been achieved, and eventually extend its borders. This instrument is the unique national state. But beware: this state performs its military functions of unification, defence and conquest only on condition that it simultaneously undertakes others: political, juridical, economic, and ideological. All these functions are indispensable to the unity of the nation and its operation as a market. What distinguishes a modern state – that is to say, national and hence bourgeois in Gramsci's sense – from a state like the Holy Roman Empire, and the innumerable mini-states of Machiavelli's Italy, is its historical task: the struggle against particularisms, even those of city-states that are highly developed economically, politically and ideologically, but doomed to collapse because of their meagre markets and urban rivalries. It is the institution of the initial forms of economic, political, juridical and ideological unification of the nation – naturally through acute class conflicts and significant contradictions. This historical task was begun in a number of countries between the fourteenth and eighteenth centuries by a specific form of state: the absolutist monarchical state. Absolutist power (more or less limited by 'basic laws', *parlements*, etc.) has, in historical experience, proved the appropriate form for the historical achievement of national unity. Absolutist signifies unique and centralized, but not arbitrary. If national unity cannot occur spontaneously, it cannot be constructed artificially either: otherwise it would be given over to an arbitrary, tyrannical power pursuing ends other than this unity. Hence the dual aspect of the power of the absolutist state according to Gramsci: it involves violence and coercion, but at the same time consent, and hence 'hegemony'.

From these conditions it emerges that if the nation can be constituted solely by means of a state, the modern state (i.e. the state that becomes imperative with the development of capitalism) can only be national. This implies that national unity cannot be achieved by a non-national, foreign state (until the nineteenth century, history is full of such endeavours, and they are perhaps not yet at an end).

This, then, is what Gramsci retains from Machiavelli as regards the past and even the proximate present (Italian national unity has still not been genuinely achieved). But if I have made a point of setting out these arguments, it is so that I can identify a difference. For Gramsci traverses this familiar past solely in order to illuminate not merely the present (a stage), but also the future. In the last resort, what grips Gramsci in Machiavelli is the future inherent in the past and the present.

Machiavelli had spoken of a New Prince; Gramsci refers to the Modern Prince. Machiavelli's Prince is an absolute sovereign to whom history assigns a decisive 'task': 'giving shape' to an already existing 'material', a matter aspiring to its form – the nation. Machiavelli's New Prince is thus a specific political form charged with executing the historical demands 'on the agenda': the constitution of a nation. Gramsci's Modern Prince is likewise a specific political form, a specific means enabling modern history to execute its major 'task': revolution and the transition to a classless society. Gramsci's Modern Prince is the Marxist–Leninist proletarian party. It is no longer a single individual, and history is no longer at the mercy of this individual's *virtù*. In Machiavelli's time, the individuality of the ruler was the requisite historical form for the constitution of a state capable of achieving national unity. The form and the objectives have since changed. To take up Lenin's expression, what is 'on the agenda' is no longer national unity, but proletarian revolution and the institution of socialism. The means to this end is no longer a superior individual, but the popular masses equipped with a party that rallies the avant-garde of the working and exploited classes. Gramsci calls this avant-garde the Modern Prince. This is how, in the dark night of fascism, Machiavelli 'speaks' to Gramsci: in the future tense. And the Modern Prince then casts its light on the New Prince: Gramsci calmly writes that *The Prince* is a 'manifesto' and a 'revolutionary utopia'. For the sake of brevity, let us say 'a revolutionary utopian manifesto'.

We shall have to ponder these terms. That this manifesto is 'utopian' is something we shall return to. But that it is a revolutionary manifesto – a term Gramsci cannot use without thinking of the *Manifesto* that haunts and governs his whole life, just as it has haunted and governed the life of revolutionary militants for more than a century (i.e. the *Communist Manifesto*) – this cannot fail to hold our attention. For this simple comparison, where a beginning recommences afresh, can put us *en route* to a slightly better appreciation of why, even today, Machiavelli touches and grips us with disconcerting strength. This time the invocation of a text – the *Manifesto* – is going to plunge us into Machiavelli's own writings.

What is the singular property of Machiavelli's discourse signalled by Gramsci when he remarks of *The Prince* that it is a revolutionary utopian manifesto? I would gladly say: it is, in the sequence of Machiavelli's reflections, a quite specific dispositive [*dispositif*] that establishes particular relations between the discourse and its 'object', between the discourse and its 'subject'.

To understand this specific difference, we must set up what it differs from and, to this end, resume the three phases of our preceding reflections.

When Machiavelli writes in black and white that he has entered upon an untrodden path, that he has founded a science, the authentic knowledge of history, rulers and peoples – the science of 'politics', to use a conventional term – we are tempted to take him literally and conceive his own pronouncements in universal categories: those of the sciences with which we are familiar, or of the 'philosophy' that follows them like their shadow. Were that the case, Machiavelli would have produced an objective and universal discourse treating, if not the 'laws of history', then the 'laws of politics', and so on. And, in certain respects, this is indeed what he imparts to us when he evokes the cycle of governmental forms, their eternal return and degeneration, the dialectic between customs and laws, laws and institutions, the constancy of human nature and the effects of its desire, and so forth. We are then dealing with the ordered exposition of abstract and universal categories, whose correlation unearths the invariants (can we say laws?) under which the particular variations of a concrete object called politics are subsumed. One often thinks of Montesquieu and his project: 'I have set down the principles, and I have seen *particular cases* conform to them as if by themselves, the histories of all nations being but their *consequences*, and each particular law connecting with another law.'[11] One thinks of him all the more in that for Montesquieu, as for Machiavelli, the objectivity and universality of scientific discourse are founded upon actual reality, not the imaginary. Does not Montesquieu also say: 'I have drawn my principles not from my prejudices, but from the nature of things'? Machiavelli's discourse, then, would be similar to that of Montesquieu: objective *because* universal, stating the laws of its object, the concrete instance of the object affording only a particular case of this universal. Let us for the time being say: a discourse 'without a subject', like any other scientific discourse – without a subject, and hence without an addressee. Were this the case, Croce – among others – would not have been wrong: Machiavelli stated the objective laws of politics much as others have elaborated those of fencing. Anyone can make use of them!

This argument, however, comes up against a difficulty that precisely makes for Machiavelli's singularity. For if a theory is indeed present in his work, it proves extremely difficult – even impossible – to state it systematically, in the form of the universality of the concept it should, however, assume. Paradoxically, if it is clear that we are confronted with theoretical thought of great rigour, the central point where everything is tied up endlessly escapes detection. It is impossible to provide a systematic, non-contradictory and complete exposition of a theory presented strangely, in the form of fragments of a whole that has been deemed 'unfinished' (Croce), but instead seems absent – and fragments arranged in a strangely deformed space, constructed in such a fashion that it is not possible to encompass or hold them together in perfect unity. As if, in Machiavelli's form of thought, there were something that eludes the rules of convention. This experience, open to anyone on the basis of the texts themselves, compels us to cast doubt on our initial idea, and to ask whether these texts do not possess a mode of existence quite different from the statement of 'laws of history'.

By way of example, let us look again at the reaction of Hegel, who may serve as a first witness. What fascinated Hegel is that Machiavelli posed a political problem that spoke to him: the problem of the constitution of a state, or – to avoid Hegelian speculation – the problem of the constitution of national unity by a national state. If this *encounter* occurs, and on this very

specific 'object', we may presume that the main thing about
Machiavelli – what gripped Hegel – is not universal history, or
even politics in general. Rather, it is a definite concrete object,
and a very peculiar 'object' (but is it still an object?) – the
formulation of a political problem: the political problem of the
concrete practice of the formation of national unity by a national
state. The affinities of the historical conjuncture that 'wanders'
between the Italian sixteenth century and the very beginning of
the German nineteenth century facilitate the Hegelian revival of
Machiavelli. We then appreciate that Machiavelli is a different
thinker from Montesquieu. What interests him is not 'the nature
of *things*' in general (Montesquieu),[12] but (to give the expression
all its force) '*la verità effettuale* della *cosa*', of *the* thing in the
singular – the singularity of its 'case'. And *the* thing is also *the*
cause, *the* task, the singular problem to be posed and resolved.
In this minor difference we can discern what shifts and separates
the whole discourse. Yes, Machiavelli's object is knowledge of
the laws of history or politics; but at the same time, this is not
the case. For his object, which is not an object in this sense, is the
formulation of a concrete political problem. Formulation of the
problem of political practice is at the heart of everything: all the
theoretical elements (as many 'laws' as you like) are arranged as
a function of this central political problematic. We can now
understand why Machiavelli does not have all the 'laws' intervene, and why he does not offer a general and systematic
exposition, but deploys only the theoretical fragments conducive
to clarification of the formulation and understanding of this
singular concrete case. So much for the fragments (and hence the
contradictions as well). Above all, however, a *theoretical dispositive* is here brought to light that breaks with the habits of classical
rhetoric, where the universal governs the singular.

Yet this recasting still remains 'theoretical'. No doubt the
order of things has been 'moved', and the formulation and
meditation of a particular political problem substituted for general knowledge of an object. But what is to stop this particular
problem being considered in its turn as the case of a general
law? What is to stop us regarding the arrangement of the
theoretical fragments focused on this particular problem as the
effect of a theoretical necessity? What is to prevent us saying, as
some Marxists would be tempted to say, that had Machiavelli

had at his disposal a scientific general theory of history, which he could not found, he could have related the theoretical fragments, deployed to the best of his ability but in a vacuum, to a general theory, whether of the state or politics? But were we to reason thus, or even allow ideology to reason on our behalf, we would run the risk of missing what is most precious in Machiavelli.

To grasp the true character of this dispositive (theoretical fragments focused on the formulation of a political problem) and its effects, we must jump a step: abandon a conception that brings in only theory for one that brings in practice and, since we are dealing with politics, political practice. This is where Gramsci's remark that *The Prince* has the character of a manifesto is going to enlighten us.

In effect, through the examination of a political problem Machiavelli offers us something quite different from the examination of a theoretical problem. By that I mean that his relationship[13] [to the political problem in question is not theoretical, but *political*. And by political relationship I mean not a relationship of political theory, but one of political *practice*. For Machiavelli it is a necessity of political practice itself that this relationship involve elements of political theory. But it is the viewpoint of *political practice* alone that fixes the modality of the relationship to the elements of political theory, and the modality and dispositive of the elements of political theory itself.]

We must therefore bring to light a new determination, hitherto passed over in silence – political practice – and say that the theoretical elements are focused on Machiavelli's concrete political problem *only because this political problem is itself focused on political practice*. As a result, political practice makes its sudden appearance in the theoretical universe where initially the science of politics in general, and then a particular political problem, were at issue. Obviously, it is a question of sudden appearance *in a text*. To be more precise, a theoretical text is affected in its modality and dispositive by political practice. What, concretely, does this mean?

To start with, it means that Machiavelli does not pose the political problem of national unity in general, even as a particular theoretical problem (among others in general); he poses this problem in terms of the case, and hence the *singular conjuncture*.[14]

I believe it is not hazardous to venture that Machiavelli is the first theorist of the conjuncture or the first thinker consciously, if not to think the concept of conjuncture, if not to make it the object of an abstract and systematic reflection, then at least consistently – in an insistent, extremely profound way – to think *in* the conjuncture: that is to say, in its concept of an aleatory, singular case.[15]

What does it mean *to think in the conjuncture?* To think about a political problem under the category of conjuncture? It means, first of all, taking account of all the determinations, all the existing concrete *circumstances,* making an inventory, a detailed breakdown and comparison of them. For example, as we can see in *The Prince* and the *Discourses,* it is insistently to revert to the division, the parcellization, of Italy – to the extreme misery into which it is plunged by wars between rulers and republics, by the Pope's intervention, by the recourse to foreign monarchs. But it is at the same time to compare and contrast with these circumstances the existence and impetuous development of the great national monarchies coeval with Italy, those of France and Spain.

This inventory of elements and circumstances, however, is insufficient. To think *in terms of* the category of conjuncture is not to think *on* the conjuncture, as one would reflect on a set of concrete data. To think under the conjuncture is quite literally to submit to the problem induced and imposed by its case:[16] the political problem of national unity and the constitution of Italy into a national state. Here the terms must be inverted: Machiavelli does not think the problem of national unity in terms of the conjuncture; it is the conjuncture itself that negatively, yet objectively, poses the problem of Italian national unity. Machiavelli merely registers in his theoretical position a problem that is objectively, historically posed by the case[17] of the conjuncture: not by simple intellectual comparisons, but by the confrontation of existing class forces and their relationship of uneven development – in fact, by their aleatory future.[18]

Now, why is Italy faced with this problem? Not only as a result of its extreme division and misery – that is to say, because Italy has not found a solution to it – but because the problem has already been posed and resolved elsewhere, in France and Spain, where the solution exists. In Machiavelli's countless comparisons between the condition of France and that of Italy, we are dealing with something quite different from simple descriptions: namely, an uneven development, a genuine difference that poses the problem of Italy and fixes its historical task.[19] The conjuncture is thus no mere summary of its elements, or enumeration of diverse circumstances, but *their contradictory system*, which poses the political problem and indicates its historical solution, *ipso facto* rendering it a political objective, a practical task.

Therewith, in next to no time, the meaning of all the elements of the conjuncture changes: they become real or potential forces in the struggle for the historical objective, and their relations become *relations of force*. They are assessed as relations of force, as a function of their engagement, with a view to the political objective to be attained. The whole question then becomes: in what *form* are all the positive forces currently available to be rallied, in order to achieve the political objective of national unity? Machiavelli gives this *form* a name: the Prince. An exceptional individual, endowed with *virtù*, who, starting from nothing or from something, will be able to mobilize the forces required to unify Italy under his leadership. There is nothing astonishing about the fact that this form is valorous *individuality*. For once again, the history that poses the problem proposes its solution, in the shape of the absolute monarchs who have succeeded in France and Spain, or the son of a Pope – Cesare Borgia – who missed his destiny and that of Italy by a mere nothing, because he wavered between life and death for a month after riding in the marshes.[20]

Once the problem has been posed and the form of its solution identified – that is to say, once the objective and the political form of its realization (i.e. the Prince) have been fixed – it only remains to define the political practice conducive to the Prince's success: the forms, means and procedures of his practice. This is the object of *The Prince* and the *Discourses*.

Let us halt for a moment. We can clearly see the way in which the modality of the object has changed. We are no longer dealing with the mythical pure objectivity of *the laws* of history or politics. Not that they have disappeared from Machiavelli's discourse. Quite the reverse: he does not cease to invoke them, and track them in their infinite variations, so as to make them declare themselves; and this 'hunt' has some surprises in store. But the theoretical truths thus produced are produced only under the stimulus of the conjuncture; and no sooner are they produced than they are affected in their modality by their intervention in a conjuncture wholly dominated by the political problem it poses, and the political practice required to achieve the objective it proposes. The upshot is what might be called a strange *vacillation* in the traditional philosophical status of these theoretical propositions: as if they were undermined by another instance than the one that produces them – the instance of political practice.

We shall see the repercussions, readable as they are, produced by this effect at the very level of theory in Machiavelli. To use a metaphorical language – but what is not metaphorical in a language that has to translate a displacement? – let us say that they are compelled to 'shift' because they are compelled *to change their space*. Assuming that it exists, the space of pure theory contrasts with the space of political practice. To sum up this difficulty, it might very schematically be said, in terms that should be transformed, that the first – theoretical – space has no subject (the truth is valid for any and every subject); whereas the second possesses meaning only via its possible or requisite subject, be it Machiavelli's New Prince or Gramsci's Modern Prince. Leaving aside the ambiguous term *subject*, which it would be advisable to replace by the term *agent*, let us say that the present space of an analysis of the political conjuncture, in its very texture, comprising opposed and intermingled forces, makes sense only if it arranges or contains a certain place, a certain *empty* place: empty in order to be filled, empty so as to have inserted in it the action of the individual or group who will come and take a stand there, so as to rally, to constitute the forces capable of accomplishing the political task assigned by history – empty for the future. I say empty, though it is always occupied. I say empty, to mark the vacillation of *theory* at this point: because it is necessary for this place to be *filled* – in other words, for the individual or party to have the capacity to become sufficiently strong to count among the forces, and strong enough again to rally the allied forces, to become the principal force and overcome the others. We can measure all the distance that separates the conception of theoretical space, or even the technical conception of politics, on this point by reference to the declaration of Descartes who, following Archimedes, required just one *fixed* point in order to shift the earth.[21] This point had to be fixed. The point demanded by the New Prince or the Modern Prince precisely cannot be a fixed point. First of all, it is not a *point* that can be localized in space, for the space of politics has no points and is only figuratively a space; at the very most, it has *places* where men are grouped under relations. And supposing that this place is a point, it would not be fixed, but mobile – better still, unstable in its very being, since all its effort must tend towards *giving itself existence*: not a transient existence – that of an individual or a sect – but historical existence – that of an absolute monarch or a revolutionary party. From this I conclude that what makes the space of political practice so different from the space of theory is that once it is submitted to the analysis of the conjuncture posing the political problem 'on the agenda' (as Lenin put it), it is *recast* in its modality and disposition by the existence of this place which is empty because it is to be filled, occupied by the 'subject' (agent) of political practice: Prince or party.

It will be appreciated that this dispositive could profoundly affect Machiavelli's discourse, and possibly provide us with the key to the strange status of theory in his writings, and all the related peculiarities.

However, we have not done with this unusual space. Indeed, there is not only one empty place in this space, but *two*. Here we come to Gramsci's remark on the *Manifesto*.

In effect, everything that has just been said plays on an ambiguity. We have spoken of the conjuncture, the relations of force that determine it, the political problem it poses, the Prince or party that must become a force to resolve it (and we constantly bore in mind the situation of Machiavelli's Italy). We have quite simply neglected the fact that the theses we have evoked are recorded in a *written* text, signed by Machiavelli, in 1513. We have simply neglected the fact that the political practice to which Machiavelli refers is not his own, but *someone else's* – this Prince summoned with wishes that are always disappointed, who will not appear before Cavour pushes a colourless personality on to the historical stage in the mid nineteenth century. Let us ignore this historical delay; it does not make the slightest difference. It remains true that everything we have noted happens in a *text*, and the question posed is the relationship between this text and the space of political practice it deploys. In other words, what place does Machiavelli's text – or, if one prefers, his written intervention – occupy in the space of political practice that it deploys? It is thus that we first discover that there is not only one place involved – the place of the 'subject' of political practice – but a second: the place of the text which politically deploys or stages this political practice.

As we can see, the question concerns a dual place or space, or a double encirclement. For Machiavelli's text to be politically effective – that is to say, for it to be, in its own fashion, the agent of the political practice it deploys – *it must be inscribed somewhere in the space of this political practice.*

I carefully clarify the question as follows: here is a text that analyses the conjuncture of Italy at the beginning of the sixteenth century. This conjuncture poses the problem of Italian national unity as the obvious historical task; and it identifies the Prince and his political practice as the means of achieving this main objective. I have indicated that the essential result of this way of posing the problem, this political problematic, cannot but be profoundly to recast the dispositive and classical modality of the theory brought into play in it. Granted. But I now add a supplementary question: how does the written text, which mobilizes and deploys this political problematic and this new dispositive, *deploy itself in the space of the problematic of political practice laid out by it?*

The first temptation is precisely to regard the text as existing outside any space. This is the thesis of the *Aufklärung*: like light, truth has no location; it occurs, and works through the efficacy of the true, whose essence is to take effect by enlightening. This could be Machiavelli's temptation when he proclaims that he is entering upon an 'untrodden path'; yet it is never to lapse into the theory of the efficacy of the 'truth'. Machiavelli knows that there is no truth – or rather, nothing true – other than what is *actual*, that is to say, borne by its effects, nonexistent outside them; and that the effectivity of the true is always merged with the activity of men; and that, politically speaking, it exists only in the confrontation between forces, the struggle between parties.[22]

This is why we must apply the rule of the 'actual truth of the thing' to the manifesto, and recognize that it is no more than a *text*. But not a text like others: it is a text which belongs to the world of ideological and political literature, which takes sides and a stand in that world. Better, a text that is an impassioned appeal for the political solution it heralds. This is enough to recast not only the standard dispositive of discourses, but also their *composition*. A 'manifesto' demands to be written in new literary forms. This explains Gramsci's admiration for the format and style of *The Prince*. For the appeal to the New Prince, a new format – barely eighty pages – and a new style: lucid, compact, vigorous and impassioned.

Why impassioned? Because Machiavelli – who never ceased to take sides in the organization of the theoretico-political dispositive of the political problem to which he proposes a solution, and who always thought the conjuncture in terms of conflicts between forces – must openly declare himself partisan in his writings, and do so with all the resources of rhetoric and passion *required to win partisans to his cause*. It is in this first sense that his text is a manifesto. He devotes all his powers as a writer to the service of the cause for which he declares. He explicitly engages in the ideological battle on behalf of the political party he supports. To put it another way: Machiavelli, who in his text elaborated the theory of the means at the disposal of the Prince set to save Italy, *treats his own text, in its turn and at the same time, as one of those means*, making it serve as a means in the struggle he announces and engages. In order to announce a New Prince in his text, he writes in a way that is suitable to the news he announces, in a novel manner. His writing is new; it is a *political act*.

The main thing, however, has yet to be said. The most important thing is not to note that the place of literature or ideology is necessarily different from that of politics, but to discover what their comparison discloses. It is here that Gramsci's remark to the effect that *The Prince* is a revolutionary *utopian* manifesto is going to assume its full significance.

For if we respect the logic of what has just been said, it would seem we must conclude that the place of the text in literature (or ideology) quite simply represents the displacement, the transfer, of the place of political practice into another element: namely, ideology. To make the same point more directly, it would seem that Machiavelli should, in ideology, *write his text from the viewpoint of the one who is to revolutionize the historical conjuncture: the Prince.* Yet we observe with astonishment that this conclusion is denied by Machiavelli himself. Let us listen to him in the 'Dedicatory Letter' of *The Prince*:

> I hope it will not be considered presumptuous for a man of very low and humble condition to dare to discuss princely government, and to lay down rules about it. For those who draw maps *place themselves on low ground, in order to understand the character of the mountains and other high points,* and climb higher in order to understand the character of the plains. *Likewise, one needs to be a ruler to understand properly the character of the people, and to be a man of the people to understand properly the character of rulers.*[23]

Machiavelli could not have represented the *space* of political practice depicted in his text any better, or gone further in recognizing the need to fix therein the place where his own text is inserted. Machiavelli's text delineates a topological space, and assigns the place – the τοποζ – that it must occupy in this space for it to become active therein, for it to constitute a political act – an element in the practical transformation of this space.

Now, what is quite remarkable is that the place fixed upon by Machiavelli for his text, the place of his *viewpoint, is not the Prince,* who is nevertheless determined as the 'subject' of the decisive political practice, *but the people.* The paradox is that in the dedication to a ruler, Lorenzo de' Medici, which opens a book that is going to speak of the Prince, Machiavelli does not hesitate to declare that 'one needs to be . . . a man of the people to understand properly the character of rulers' – hence, not to be a ruler. This means not only that rulers are incapable of knowing themselves, but that *there can be no knowledge of rulers except from the viewpoint of the people.* (Although we cannot be certain, the related assertion that there can be no knowledge of peoples except from the viewpoint of rulers may be seen as a clever way of qualifying this. For Machiavelli does not claim to discuss the people, and did not write a manifesto entitled *The People*.) But we must go further: Machiavelli does not say that one needs to be a man of the people to know the nature of *the* Prince, but the nature of *princes* – implying that there are several sorts, and thus that there is a choice to be made between them *from the viewpoint of the people.*

Machiavelli could not declare his partisanship, affirm his class position, more firmly. It is no accident that he begins by recalling the 'very low and humble condition' that makes him belong to the people. *Class membership* ('class-being': Mao) is not enough. To it he adds the declaration of his *class position*, his class viewpoint. Outside this class position, his enterprise and his writings are inexplicable: to speak of the Prince as he does, one needs to be a man of the people, aligned with the class positions of the people. This is what Gramsci says: in his manifesto, Machiavelli 'becomes the people'.[24]

This yields two results. First, it enables us to understand the meaning of his whole discourse on the Prince and the state. Machiavelli does not want just any ruler: this theorist of the sovereign power of one man is the most radical enemy of every tyranny. This theorist of the state is not – as Hegel believed – a theorist of *the* state, but of the *national* state, or – as Gramsci puts it – *of national unity by means of the popular state.* The second result is that Machiavelli, who addresses the Prince with desperation, does so *from the viewpoint of the people.* Under the guise of the Prince, it is in fact the people he is addressing. This manifesto, which seems to have for its sole interlocutor a future individual, an individual who does not exist, is in fact addressed to the mass of the common people. A manifesto is not written for an individual, especially a nonexistent individual: it is always addressed to the masses, in order to organize them into a revolutionary force.[25]

The undeniable fact nevertheless remains that Machiavelli did not write a text comparable to the *Communist Manifesto.*

The *Communist Manifesto* is likewise a written text that arranges social classes in the space of economic, political and ideological class struggle; a text that poses theoretically the problem posed socially and politically by the conjuncture – social revolution – and fixes the place of the force that must be constituted to resolve this problem – that is to say, make the revolution. This place is the proletariat; and this force is the party of the proletariat.

Of course, the *Communist Manifesto,* too, is a written text. As such, it occupies a *place* in the ideological literature of the time, as we can see in the section where Marx and Engels make an inventory of existing socialist literature, so that they can resolutely demarcate themselves from it.[26] This written text thus locates itself in political ideology, which occupies a specific place in the space of the political topology laid out by the *Manifesto*, with all the consequences this involves for the theoretical dispositive, format and literary form of the *Manifesto* itself.

There is thus a *distinction* between the *place* of political ideology in which the *Manifesto* is consciously situated and the kind of effect the intervention of a text written in that place can produce, on the one hand, and the *place* of proletarian economic and political class struggle, and the effects of this struggle, on the other. A manifesto is not a leaflet; a manifesto or leaflet is not a strike, a demonstration, or an insurrection. Yet if these places are *distinct*, they are not *different* in the case of the *Communist Manifesto*. Indeed, the *Manifesto* locates itself on the positions of the proletariat, but to summon that same proletariat and the other exploited classes to organize themselves into the party of the proletariat. The class viewpoint from which the *Manifesto* is conceived and composed is, in ideology, the *viewpoint* of the proletariat. Class viewpoint and class party pertain to one and the same class: the proletariat.

The same is not true of *The Prince*. Admittedly, Machiavelli adopts the viewpoint of the people. But while the Prince who is assigned the mission of unifying the Italian nation must become a *popular Prince*, he is not himself the *people*. Equally, the people are not summoned to become the Prince. So there is an irreducible duality between the *place* of the political *viewpoint* and the *place* of the political force and practice; between the 'subject' of the political viewpoint – the people – and the 'subject' of the political practice: the Prince. This duality, this irreducibility, affects *both* the Prince *and* the people. Being uniquely and exclusively defined by the function he must perform – that is to say, by the historical vacuum he must fill – the Prince is a pure aleatory possibility–impossibility.[27] No class membership disposes him to assume his historical task; no social tie binds him to this people whom he must unify into a nation. Everything hangs on his *virtù* – that is to say, the subjective conditions of his success. As for the people who expect this impossible Prince to transform them into a nation, and from whose perspective Machiavelli defines the Prince's politics, nothing obliges or even prompts them to constitute themselves as a people, to transform themselves into a people, or – *a fortiori* – to become a *political force*. Certainly, we shall see Machiavelli distinguishing with care between the feudal class, who possess and oppress without working, and the common people, who cultivate the land or make wool and iron, as well as those who trade and speculate. But this labouring and trading population is divided; and there is no indication that Machiavelli made any attempt *to overcome this division*. History must be made by the Prince from the viewpoint of the people; but the people is not yet 'the subject' of history.

This distinction justifies Gramsci's remark. *The Prince* is a kind of revolutionary manifesto, but a *utopian* one. Revolutionary, in so far as Machiavelli clearly understood the revolutionary task 'on the agenda' – the constitution of the national state – and poses this problem from *the viewpoint of the people*. But utopian in two senses. First, in so far as Machiavelli believed that the 'situation was revolutionary', and that Italy was ready to become a national and popular state. (I encapsulate the distinction in Lenin's formulation: revolution, or a historical task, can be on the agenda without the concrete situation being revolutionary.) And second, in so far as Machiavelli, for all sorts of reasons that would require detailed examination, entrusts to *someone else* – to an unknown individual whom he thought he recognized in several successive personalities, an individual indefinable in advance – the mission of achieving national unity on behalf of a third party: the people. The duality of places and 'subjects' thus results in the alterity of utopia, entrusting the realization of national unity to a mythical individual: the Prince. When Gramsci says that Machiavelli becomes the people, that he speaks to the people, to 'those who do not know'; when he writes that '[t]he entire "logical argument"' of *The Prince* 'appears as nothing other than auto-reflection on the part of the people – an inner reasoning worked out in the popular consciousness', this reflection remains utopian. For if it can contribute to modifying the political consciousness of the people, it is only to put this simple consciousness as consciousness in contact with a possible and desirable event: the advent of the Prince. It is not in order to transform this consciousness into a *political force capable of producing this event, or participating in its production.*

As is well known, the *Communist Manifesto* and the First International obviously speak a very different language. The emancipation of the workers will be achieved by the workers themselves. Workers of the world, unite. Neither God nor master. . . .

To sum up this preliminary detour, I would therefore say that there are two reasons why Machiavelli's text is simultaneously gripping and elusive, why it 'speaks' to us with such force and presence, and why it is so difficult to understand it philosophically and explain it theoretically.

The unusual character of the text consists first in the fact that although it is laden with theory, it is not a theoretical text like any other, but one in which the traditional theoretical space (traditional designates a certain ideological representation of what such a text is) is distorted, inflected, and rendered unrecognizable by an arrangement and dispositive that are connected not only with politics, not only with the historical conjuncture and its tasks, but also – and above all – with *political practice* and the *class viewpoint* it involves. This reference profoundly affects the classical modality of theory, shatters its dispositive, dismembers it, and reconstitutes it in a specific form that makes it impossible for the traditional categories of philosophy to grasp it.

The unusual character of this text consists secondly in the fact that, in Machiavelli, the places of class viewpoint and political practice are dissociated: this hiatus opens up the vacuum of utopia, which overdetermines the preceding effects. We shall have the opportunity to review the actual evidence.

But before going into detail, I should like to offer a significant example of the disconcerting effects produced by the unusual character of Machiavelli's text. That example is Rousseau. In his way, he can sum up the whole problem Machiavelli's text poses to its readers.

As is well known, as soon as it was published, *The Prince* elicited the most violent condemnations from those whom Marx dubbed 'professional ideologues' – clergymen and moralists – for reasons that earned Machiavelli the rare historical privilege of coining an adjective: Machiavellian. This is an adjective that indicates not agreement (whether with Machiavelli's work or

thought: Machiavellian [*machiavélien*] in the same way as one
would say 'Kantian'); but, rather, a quality (Machiavellian
[*machiavélique*], as one would say 'Platonic' or 'Dantesque') –
and, moreover, a 'derogatory' one. The reason is that Machiavelli
makes religion an instrument of politics, subordinates morality
to political practice, and – to go to extremes – defends the
Prince's right, in certain circumstances, to resort to cruelty, guile,
bad faith, and so on.[28] The Jesuits made themselves notorious by
declaring that *The Prince* had been written 'with the Devil's
hand', and that its author was 'the supreme craftsman of the
Devil's thoughts'. But these reactions are of little interest.[29] More
significant are those that concern Machiavelli's actual object –
politics – and his partisanship in the political struggle. *The Prince*
has sometimes elicited praise from statesmen (like Richelieu and
Napoleon, who nevertheless said that Machiavelli discusses war
like someone who is colour-blind); and sometimes provoked
denunciation – for example, from the Huguenots, whose co-
religionists were massacred on Saint Bartholomew's Eve; and
Frederick II of Prussia, author of an *Anti-Machiavelli* that was
soon suspected of serving to cover the very practices from which
he publicly distanced himself by their denial.

Be that as it may, this whole dispute over Machiavelli – his
political adoption and condemnation alike – brought to light *the*
question of the political meaning of his *œuvre*, in directly paradoxical terms. And not by chance.

The question cannot but be formulated as follows: considering
this written text that is *The Prince*; considering that it is devoted
to the Prince (in the singular), if not every ruler; considering that
it sets out what the Prince (any ruler) must do, how he must
conduct himself and proceed in order to found and expand his
state, using all available means, regardless of their compatibility
with individual morality and the prevailing religion – *whom*,
then, does this work serve? The first thought that comes to mind
is that this treatise on *The Prince* serves the Prince, or even any
prince. But if we say that this work serves the Prince, or any
prince, we immediately run up against the fact that it is a
published writing – hence *public* – which tells everyone one
man's business; and hence that at the very moment it arms the
Prince with its methods, it disarms him by making them public.
To be more precise, in *The Prince* and the *Discourses*, Machiavelli

also furnishes the rules to be followed to produce effects of opinion that depend, above all, on the art of dissimulation. If the whole art of ruling consists in producing controlled effects of opinion, based on a well-ordered appearance, a calculated feint, then publicizing the rules of the game, of deceit and dissimulation, the procedure and process of fraud, obviously involves a strange contradiction. From here it is only a short step to thinking that Machiavelli's text is itself a feint. In effect, Machiavelli pretends to instruct rulers. But if he claims merely to state the facts, to provide an account of their actual practice, then what can he teach them that they do not already know? Rulers have always managed on their own, and they do not need a Machiavelli. Indeed, they can only be terribly inconvenienced by this intruder who confesses their shameful conduct and makes their secret practices public. As we examine this unusual text, the suspicion then arises that this private individual, who publicly instructs rulers in the art of dissimulation and guile in the government of men, is actually governing rulers by another cunning twist which, like Pascal's twist to madness, imparts to it the most innocent air in the world.

The truth of *The Prince* then appears for what it is: a prodigious stratagem, that of the *non-stratagem*; a prodigious dissimulation, that of non-dissimulation – the great snare of the 'actual truth' set in the open for rulers to come and entrap themselves all on their own. The 'truth' on politics is a political ruse. But then, if Machiavelli brought off this amazing feat of deceiving rulers by telling them the truth that was to serve them, *whom* does this ruse of the ruse, this feint of the feint, serve? Does it simply serve the acute consciousness of a man of humble condition who, by mere virtue of writing about those whom he has had to serve, exacts a revenge enjoyed by him alone?

Here is Rousseau's response: 'He professed to teach kings; but it was the people he really taught. His *Prince* is the book of republicans.' And in a note Rousseau adds that, 'in the midst of his country's oppression', Machiavelli was compelled to 'veil [. . .] his love of liberty'; that he had a 'hidden aim' which emerges when one compares *The Prince* (apparently monarchist) with the *Discourses on Livy* (truly republican). Rousseau concludes: 'this profound political thinker has so far been studied only by superficial or corrupt readers'.[30]

How does *The Prince* serve the people? The *Encyclopédie* entry on 'Machiavellianism' (doubtless by Diderot) supplies the answer:

> When Machiavelli wrote his treatise on *The Prince*, it is as if he said to his fellow citizens: Read this work carefully. Should you ever accept a master, he will be such as I depict him for you. Here is the savage brute to whom you will be abandoning yourselves. Thus it was the fault of his contemporaries if they misjudged his aim: they took a satire for a eulogy.

This is a blatant misinterpretation, whose immediate cause is the interval and superimposition of times, historical conjunctures, and the effects of displacement and redistribution of roles it induces in the reading and estimate of the text. But this interval and superimposition do not explain everything. Why this passion for Machiavelli? Why, apart from the 'corrupt' ones, should this extremely 'profound' politician have had only *superficial* readers? Why this misconstrual of a satire as a eulogy? Why, if they were superficial, should his readers have been so gripped by Machiavelli that he has remained of the utmost *presence*, and an altogether peculiar presence, since – wholly superficial as his readers may be – his text has the remarkable property of passionately dividing them over its interpretation?

It is impossible to answer this question if *Machiavelli's specific arrangement of theoretical and political space* is not taken into account. Indeed, Machiavelli's text is so arranged that it is impossible not, in one way or another, consciously or unconsciously, to be struck by the question: *for whom* was this text written, and *from what viewpoint* was it conceived? This question is silently imposed by the dispositive of Machiavelli's revolutionary utopian manifesto, through the existence of the two alternate 'places' that govern its forms of presentation, argumentation, and theoretical reflection: the Prince and the People.

To retain only the Prince, without realizing that he is thought *from the viewpoint of the people,* is to lapse into 'Machiavellianism': the recipes of tyranny and villainy. But – and this is the effect of the people's presence – it is, by the same token, to fall into the contradiction of the feint of the feint: the treatise on *The Prince* backfires on the Prince, and the addressee disappears with the address. To retain only the people, as in the so-called 'democratic' interpretation, is to unmask the Prince, but to fall into the contradiction of denouncing a Prince who is simultaneously called upon to accomplish the great work of Italian unity; and this is the effect of the Prince's presence.

I therefore conclude that these alternate effects are not merely the product of interpretations elaborated from a viewpoint external to the text, but the reflection, in external interpretations, of the *double viewpoint* internal to the text, which functions not as a series of theoretical statements, not as the exposition of a solution, but as the formulation of a political problem, as an *interrogation*, as the matrix of a political problem that divides protagonists on the conception of the conditions of *political practice*.

If all these remarks are not unwarranted, we can appreciate why Machiavelli is simultaneously gripping and elusive. It is precisely because he is gripping that he cannot be grasped by traditional philosophical thought. He is gripping because – as much as any writing can – his text practically, politically, implicates and involves us. He hails us from a place that he summons us to occupy as potential 'subjects' (agents) of a potential political practice. This effect of captivation and interpellation is produced by the shattering of the traditional theoretical text, by the sudden appearance of the political problem as a problem and of the political practice in it as a practice; and by the double reflection of political practice in his text and of his text in political practice. Gramsci was the first to appreciate this. It is no accident that Gramsci, having grasped the elusiveness of Machiavelli, could understand him, and that he discusses him in a text of which Merleau-Ponty might likewise have inquired: 'How could he have been understood?' In fact, Gramsci, too, is elusive, for the same reasons that render Machiavelli elusive to us.

Theory and Theoretical Dispositive in Machiavelli

We are now going to attend to the texts and examine the evidence of how theory is presented in Machiavelli: we are going to analyse his *theoretical dispositive*.

Everything I have just suggested seems to be contradicted by the existence of a theory of history in Machiavelli, by which we mean a *general theory of the laws of history*. No doubt this is a new theory, proclaimed in the preface to the *Discourses* when Machiavelli writes: 'I have resolved to enter upon a path *still untrodden*'.[1] How is it new? In so far as it goes directly to 'things as they are in actual truth, rather than as they are imagined'. Hence it is positive, shorn of any religious, moral or aesthetic representation.

But representing things as they actually are is insufficient: knowledge of things, of their 'laws', is required. How does Machiavelli produce this new theory of history? By means of a new method: an *experimental* method. In *The Prince* Machiavelli says that if he can write his book, it is because he has been educated '*by long experience* of modern affairs and continual study of ancient history'.[2] This experimentation is conducted via the *comparison* of what Machiavelli calls 'ancient and modern events and circumstances'.[3] Through this comparison he obtains 'a true understanding of history'.[4] In a moment we shall see the meaning of this experimental comparison.

Now, the remarkable thing is that this experimental comparison of 'events and circumstances' refers to a general theory of the '*laws*' of history. How is this to be construed? Is the general theory of history the result of experimental comparisons, or are the 'laws of history' their precondition? This question is crucial. To convey its importance, we shall speak of *theses* on universal history, rather than *laws* of history. What are the theses of this general theory?

First thesis. The course of natural and human things is immutable: '. . . as if the sky, the sun, the elements, or human beings had changed in their motions, order, and power from what they were in antiquity'.[5] And in Book I, Chapter 39 of the *Discourses*, Machiavelli writes: 'Anyone who studies current and ancient affairs will easily recognize that the same desires and humours exist and have always existed in all cities and among all peoples . . . it . . . follows that the same conflicts arise in every era.'[6] The world does not change. In the Preface to Book II of the *Discourses*, Machiavelli specifies: 'As I reflect upon how these affairs proceed, I conclude that the world has always been in the same state, and that . . . there has always been as much good as evil in it.'[7]

What is the significance of this first thesis? It might appear opposed in its very letter to any revolutionary project: if the world is immutable, how can it be changed? We shall see Machiavelli's answer to this question. For now, let us be content with a simple observation bearing upon the extreme generality of the thesis. To use a language different from Machiavelli's, I would say that this thesis is remarkable not only for its extreme generality, but also for its theoretical status.[8] In fact, it functions not as a theoretico-scientific proposition on history but, rather, as a *philosophical thesis*: on the one hand, a thesis about the objectivity and universality of the forthcoming scientific propositions; on the other, a thesis founding the possibility of the experimental comparisons between 'cases'[9] Machiavelli is going to make to produce his theoretical propositions. Were the human world not *the same*, it would not be possible to make comparisons between antiquity and the present – on the one hand, between the diverse events and conjunctures of antiquity; on the other, between the diverse events and conjunctures of the present (Italy and France, say); and finally, between these two orders of conjuncture. If it were not the same – constant – it would not be possible to isolate the constants – the 'laws' – or, rather, their 'invariants'; it would not be possible to know it.[10]

Second thesis. This positively contradicts the first:

> [S]ince all human affairs are in continual motion and cannot remain fixed, they must either rise or fall, and reason does not always lead you to the many things to which necessity leads you, so that if a republic were to be capable of maintaining itself without expansion, and necessity forced it to expand, its foundations would be demolished and it would be brought to ruin very quickly.[11]

So everything is in continual, unstable motion, subject to an unpredictable necessity. This necessity is represented by the mythical conceptual figure of Fortune. The vogue of Fortune, to whom the Romans built a temple, has been revived 'in our own times', Machiavelli writes in *The Prince*, 'because of the great changes that have taken place and are still to be seen even now, which could hardly have been predicted'.[12] In countless places in *The Prince* and the *Discourses*, fortune is described as liable to unpredictable changes – for example, when a ruler is advised to 'be prepared to vary his conduct as the winds of fortune and changing circumstances constrain him'.[13] Its law is change, and this law sums up the law of historical time, hence of history: times change, conjunctures change, men change. 'All human affairs' are therefore 'in continual motion'. We shall say of this second law that it, too, is a philosophical thesis, this time founding not the possibility of an objective knowledge of history and the comparative experimental method, but the possibility of comparative variations on the one hand, and the possibility of revolution on the other. To anticipate once again as regards terminology, following the equivalent of a materialist thesis, this time we have the equivalent of a 'dialectical' or, rather, *'aleatory'* thesis.[14]

Third thesis. If, retaining their sense as *positive* propositions on history (rather than as philosophical theses), we go on to compare the letter of the first two theses, they are contradictory: continual change is contrasted with the immutable order of things, immobility. This contradiction requires a solution. Machiavelli furnishes it in the synthesis of the immutable order of things with their continual change: in a *cyclical* theory of history. This is presented at the beginning of the *Discourses*.[15] Taken directly from Polybius, it is a theory of the necessary *cycle* human history endlessly undergoes in passing from one form of government to another; a theory of the cycle – and no longer a typology – of governments, categorized under two rubrics: the good and the bad.

Here is the cycle (I summarize its essentials). '[I]n the beginning of the world ... variations in governments arise among men by chance.' Human beings are 'few', 'scattered like beasts'. '[A]s the generations multiplied they gathered together, and in order better to defend themselves, they began to consider carefully who among them was stronger and braver.' This was 'the era of combination into society'. Conflicts immediately arose between men, who 'set about making laws in order to avoid similar evils'. This was the origin of justice, which influenced the choice of leader: 'they did not support the boldest but, instead, the man who was most prudent and just.' This was the first form of government: *monarchy* (1).

I open a parenthesis to make two observations. The first is to underscore the thesis, seemingly unimportant when stated in passing, that at the origin of all governments (and, before them, every society) we find *chance*, which we cannot but relate to fortune in some way. To say that chance is at the origin of societies and governments, and to say that at the outset human beings were scattered – dispersion is inherent in chance, from Democritus and Epicurus up to Rousseau in the *Second Discourse* – is obviously to reject any anthropological ontology of society and politics.[16] In particular, it is to reject the theory of Aristotle (that great absentee from Machiavelli's thought) according to which man is 'by nature' a political animal. But it is also – and this is my second observation – to reject (unlike Epicurus) any *contractual* theory of the origin of society and government. Machiavelli is one of those political theorists who do without the social contract. He says that the masses elected the most powerful and promised him obedience, but makes no mention of a reciprocal contract. What is more, laws postdate the beginning of society, postdate government by the most powerful, but predate the establishment of monarchy. It is no accident that Machiavelli allots this eminent place to juridical and political laws.[17] We shall see why when the time comes.

We have witnessed the birth of monarchy. It is going to

degenerate into *tyranny*. The heirs of the ruler lose his virtue, sinking into decadence and indolence. Hence the hatred of their subjects. The king takes fright at this hatred, reacting with the instruments of fear: arbitrariness and violence.

Machiavelli observes that the ensuing disorders issue not from the people, but from the nobles. The nobles rebel against the king; the people follow them and overthrow him. The nobles then take power: this is *aristocracy* (2), which is also going to degenerate – into *oligarchy*, which is also tyrannical. In and through the same process, the successors of the first aristocrats in power induce the degeneration of aristocratic government: they forget the virtues of their fathers, incite the hatred of the people, and then turn against the people by becoming tyrants.

The people once again rebel against their new masters. Since all other solutions have been exhausted, there remains only *democracy* (3). The same process recurs: the successors of the first government lose the virtue of their ancestors. They arouse the people's hatred with their excesses or their carelessness. Democratic government degenerates into 'licence'. The people rebel and seek a new master, who will be a king. The cycle is now complete.

And the same cycle is going to recommence: monarchy degenerating into tyranny; aristocracy degenerating into tyrannical oligarchy; and democracy degenerating into anarchy:

> [T]his is the cycle through which all states [i.e. all peoples constituted into states] ... pass, but rarely do they return to the same forms of government, because almost no republic can be so full of life that it may pass through these mutations many times and remain standing. But it may well happen that in the course of its troubles, a republic ever lacking in counsel and strength becomes subject to a nearby state that is better organized; but if this were not to occur, a republic would be apt to circle about endlessly through these types of government.[18]

Such, in its simplicity, is the cyclical theory of history, the typology of governments, as partially borrowed by Machiavelli from Polybius. By means of the third thesis on the cyclical character of history, Machiavelli seems to have achieved, brought off, a 'synthesis', in the vulgar-Hegelian sense, between the first thesis (immutable order) and the second (universal mobility). What is the historical cycle if not the immobile motion, the immutable movement, of the recurrence of the same changes?

It seems as if we have arrived at a conclusion, at a general theory of history that it suffices to register as such, and which has no further implications. It would appear that everything has been said: everything except the *modality* of this theory in Machiavelli's text; everything save the use Machiavelli makes of this cyclical general theory, and the theoretical function he assigns it. Acccordingly, following these three theses, we must define Machiavelli's position and stand.

A moment ago, we noted the presence of chance at the origin of societies and governments, and then the presence of laws prior to monarchy. We now note that monarchy is the first form of government. We also note that the degeneration of governments delivers them into *tyranny*, which figures here as the *bête noire* of the people *and* Machiavelli. We further observe that the rebellions inducing revolutions in the forms of government are always the deed of the people, who start hating their leaders and change them. These are only indications.

What is a lot more important is that, immediately after referring to the 'endless circle of types of government', Machiavelli declares:

> Let me say, therefore, that *all* forms of government mentioned above are *defective*, because of the brief duration of the three *good* ones, and because of the evil nature of the three *bad* ones. Thus, since those men who were prudent in establishing laws recognized this defect, they avoided each of these forms by itself alone and chose a form of government that combined them all, judging such a government steadier and more stable, for when in the same city there is a [monarchy], an aristocracy, and a democracy, one keeps watch over the other.[19]

And he compares the example of Lycurgus of Sparta, 'who organized his laws . . . in such a way that, allocating to the kings, the aristocrats, and the people their respective roles, he created a state that lasted for more than 800 years', with that of Solon in Athens, 'who by instituting only a democratic form of government there gave it such a brief existence that, before he died, he saw the tyranny of Pisistratus arise . . . [because] Solon did not mix a popular form of government with the power of the [monarchy] and that of the aristocrats, Athens endured a very brief time in comparison to Sparta'.[20]

It cannot be said that Machiavelli lets us take a breath, for this is a strange way of bringing his theory of the cycle of governments to bear! Whereas Polybius (like the whole tradition derived from Aristotle before and after him) carefully contrasted *good* governments with those *bad* governments that are the forms of their degeneration, Machiavelli pronounces them *all* defective – the bad ones because they are bad, the good ones on account of their 'brief duration'! In other words, Machiavelli has no sooner alluded to the classical problematic of the *typology* of governments than he changes terrain and problem, offering us an example and problem that transport us to a quite different world. Under the guise of the (experimental) comparison between Lycurgus as 'event' and Solon as 'event', he proposes a form of government absent from Polybius, from the typology, from the cycle – a form combining 'a popular form of government with the power of the [monarchy] and that of the aristocrats'. He presents this form of government as established by a legislator, and declares that it is the sole good one, because it is 'steadier and more stable' – in short, because it is capable of 'lasting' eight hundred years in Sparta!

For the moment, let us leave the legislator to one side. But let us retain this idea of 'duration'. Machiavelli observed that the *good* governments in the Polybian typology have a 'brief duration'. On the other hand, in the remarkable paragraph quoted above, where it is a question of the endless cycle of revolutions, Machiavelli pointed out (and this is not in Polybius either) that if states *endured* long enough, they would endlessly undergo the whole cycle of governments. However, 'no republic can be so full of life that it may pass through these mutations many times and remain standing'. Here we are concerned with the overthrow not of governments, but of *states* – that is to say, their disappearance when they are conquered by more powerful states. If these rather astonishing assertions are compared in context, we first of all discover that Machiavelli is interested not in governments as governments pure and simple – hence in simple *forms* giving rise to a typological treatment – but in governments as governments of *states*; and thus that he is interested in forms of government in so far, and only in so far, as they resolve a problem pertaining to the *state* – that is to say, *a different reality* from mere governments.

And we then discover that the fundamental problem of the state, which haunts Machiavelli in his recasting of the classical typology, is its *duration*. Machiavelli is interested in only one form of government: that which enables a state to endure.

In these conditions, if we revert to the third thesis – the cyclical theory of history – we discover that Machiavelli proposes it solely in order to demarcate himself from it while he is relying on it. Just as the thesis of continual change contradicted the thesis of the immutable order of things, so too *Machiavelli's position on the duration of the state contradicts the thesis of the endless cycle of revolutions in forms of government*. In fact, what Machiavelli wants is not a government that passes away, but a state that endures. And in order to impart and guarantee duration to it, he assigns it a 'composite' form of government that does not feature in the typology of governments in continual transition – hence an utterly *original* form of government, unlike all the forms inventoried in the typology in so far as it is *durable* and capable (we already suspect it) of rendering the state Machiavelli has in mind *durable*, whereas the recorded states are of such brief duration that the law of the historical cycle, according to which governments are not durable, cannot be verified in their case. . . . Once again, Machiavelli thus comes to deny what he has previously asserted.

What is the meaning of this new negation? And, more generally, *what is the meaning of these negations*? We have already witnessed the negation of what I called the first thesis by the second, but we have seen that this negation does not constitute a pure and simple contradiction in terms. Rather, it represents an articulation, a play, a positive determination – in the Spinozist sense – of the negation. Taken literally, the thesis of continual change contradicts the thesis of the immutable order of things. If one merely compares the formulations, it is sufficient to be a scribe or a lawyer to draft an indictment of contradiction, and to infer Machiavelli's (subjective or objective) *inconsistency*. It is well-known that this concept of inconsistency made the fortune of *Aufklärung* and Young Hegelian critique. But if things are taken not literally, but seriously in the text in which they *intervene*; if, rather than their formal literal sense, we consult their function, then we discover that it is the fact that they are *paired* – or, better, coupled, yoked – which establishes their theoretical function and brings it into play, inducing the interplay, the articulation, and thus opens up the determinate field of this theoretical function. In this way the formulation of the first thesis functions in Machiavelli's discourse as a materialist thesis of objectivity; and it is solely against its background that the formulation of the second thesis can function as an aleatory *dialectical* determination of this objectivity.[21] Without the first thesis (objectivity), the second would function merely in the sceptical mode of subjective relativism.[22] Thanks to the first, the second, which is its negation, is then its determination – that is to say, the determination of objectivity: it postulates the objectivity – in other words, the intelligibility – of *universal change*.

Similarly, we can say that the third thesis, as the negation of the second, adds a new *determination* to it: namely, that objective universal change occurs according to *forms* – those of governments – thought in the permanence of the endless cycle of revolutions. It thus represents the synthesis of the first two (the cycle), but at the price of adding consideration of these (stable/unstable) *forms*: governments.

What, then, of what might be called Machiavelli's fourth thesis, but I prefer to call his position? This in turn constitutes a negation of the third thesis, but a very peculiar negation, since it does not merely deny, but completely *displaces* it. Therewith is confirmed the idea that what interests Machiavelli is (1) not the governments of the cycle, but a quite different government; (2) not governments, but the duration of the state; and (3) not the cycle of endless recurrence, but the wish to rely on it *so as to escape it* – the will to be *emancipated* from the immutable necessity of the endless cycle of the same revolutions in order to create not a government that is going to degenerate to pave the way for its successor, but a *state that lasts*. This time the negation is not term for term – not-A as against A – but involves a disparity: it is a *positive counter-position* in which the new term is determined not by a simple formal negation but by a different content, introduced under the form of negation.

The operation can be concretely analysed as follows: (1) the endless cycle of governments is negated in the postulation of a state that endures; (2) but this state that endures is something other than the negation of the governments featuring in the cycle, *since it is a state*; (3) and its form (the triple combination) is something other than the forms featuring in the cycle, since it is a distinct form of government. Thus this new negation is very peculiar, and that is why I have not expressed it in the form of a fourth thesis, but have spoken of Machiavelli's *position*. In this position there is a significant space, a vacuum, a leap into the theoretical void, an anticipation. There comes a moment when Machiavelli can no longer 'gamble on' classical theory, or play it off against another, to open up his own space: he must leap into the void.[23] Machiavelli is no longer content to furnish the theoretical conditions of possibility for thinking his discourse on history and politics, objectivity, the aleatory 'dialectic',[24] forms in the process of development. He anticipates what he intends: *his 'object' is in fact a determinate objective.* As far as possible, he relies on what he has previously asserted in his three theses; he retains everything they provide as so many conditions, and tightens them up as much as he can. But this is in order to take the distance that is indispensable if he is to set out alone, on the 'untrodden path' he opens up. For no one has ever stated what he has in mind. To employ an unduly modern image, it might be said that Machiavelli demands from the general theory culminating in the theory of the endless cycle of revolutions the means by which to escape its gravitation, and launch himself into the uncharted space where he ventures.

But before following Machiavelli into this uncharted space, I should like to give three examples of the effects he derives from the 'play' of the theoretical dispositive I have just analysed.

First example. This involves the novel duration of the new state, this negation of the second negation – the cycle – that is itself a negation of the first – universal change. A certain isomorphism can be said to obtain between this duration and the first thesis: the universal course, the permanency, of things and men. It is not explicit; at no point does Machiavelli state it. But everything 'works' as if the existence of a durable state restored and rejoined a fundamental permanency, as if the negation of the negation (to speak a Hegelian language) restored the first affirmation – but with this difference: that here it would be a question not of the negation of the negation, but of the negation of the negation of the negation; with this fundamental difference, too, that what is involved is not the natural order of things (an existing permanency) but an order to be instituted, a duration to be fashioned, a permanency *to be established* – in short, a political undertaking and innovation. At all events, it is clear that if it does not reinstate it, this theory of the durable state is propped up on the first thesis in allusive fashion. We can thus see how the first thesis 'works': it does not simply postulate objectivity, and is not purely 'philosophical'; it also proposes a certain idea of time – it is already *political*.

Second example. This bears on a sentence that has already been quoted, which I now repeat: 'As I reflect upon how these affairs proceed, I conclude that the world has always been in much the same state, and that although there has always been as much evil as good in it, this evil and this good vary from province to province.'[25] Earlier, I failed to signal this strange final clause. The same thing happens here as in the passage on the endless cycle of revolutions: at the end of that passage Machiavelli unexpectedly inflected it, evoking the fact that states do not endure long enough to verify the 'law'. Here, too, something emerges at the end. I reiterate that we are dealing with the first thesis. The theme – 'the world has always been in the same state' – is rendered more precise: this same state is the same quantity of good and evil. This aggregate quantitative permanency is immediately negated by an internal variation: a variation in the distribution of good and evil, their historical displacement from one province to another. An extremely inter-esting idea is thus mooted. And when we see how it is justified, we find it all the more striking. What is this *good* the sum of which remains constant? It is *virtù*, a concept we shall have to discuss in detail:

> [T]his evil and good vary from province to province; this can be seen from what we know of ancient kingdoms that differed from one another according to the variations in their customs, while the world remained as it had always been. There is only this one difference, that the world first lodged its [*virtù*] in Assyria, then moved to Media, and later passed into Persia, and from there it entered Italy and Rome. If, after the Roman empire, no other empire has followed it that has endured, nor a single place in which the world has gathered together all its [*virtù*], it can be seen nevertheless that this

ability has been distributed among many nations where men live ably. . . .[26]

And Machiavelli proceeds to cite the Franks, the Turks, the Saracens, the Arabs, and France.

Here, then, is a sentence that passes directly from the first thesis (the world is always the same) to a variation, to an original and novel form of the third thesis (the general theory of the cycle), or rather, to a negation of the third thesis. This law of the conservation of the same sum of good and evil is simultaneously the law of the alteration of the point of insertion – the geographical displacement – of good and evil in history.

In truth, *there is no longer a cycle, but displacement and distribution*. It is no longer a question of the various *forms* of government, but of *virtù* and its opposite. Thus this law disregards the cycle, the regular forms of government, and their respective quality (good, bad). It concerns a quite different quality: *virtù*. What is *virtù*? We shall have occasion to return to it. But to anticipate, let us say: in Machiavelli *virtù* is quintessentially the quality specific to the *subjective* conditions for the constitution of a state that endures. This new concept, produced starting from general theses on the laws of history, is added to the new concepts acquired on the basis of the third thesis via its deferred negation: the state that endures and the combination of powers.

We thereby perceive Machiavelli's relation to his general theses, to what can be called his theory of history. By working on these theses, he so arranges them that, far from applying them as the general truth of every possible object to a particular concrete object, he *determines* them in negating them by one another. And he does so in order to make them produce, on their own theoretical basis, which plays the conjoint role of philosophical principle and conceptual matrix, concepts that it is strictly impossible to *deduce* from these theses.

Indeed, *taken literally*, these theses are contradictory, and the only effect they can have is to preclude any discourse. But if they are considered in their *arrangement*, their dispositive and their interplay, their inconsistency becomes productive of a new theoretical space and precise conceptual effects.

Take, for example, Machiavelli's assertion that *virtù* remains constant in history, while its point of application varies. This claim – built on to the first three theses, but negating the last in a specific manner – produces two effects of significance *simultaneously*. *On the one hand*, it furnishes Machiavelli with the theoretical argument for the possibility of thinking that this *virtù*, adrift in the West after experiencing its highest concentration in Rome, can and must be fixed, since all the objective conditions are assembled for it to 'take' in Italy. *And on the other hand*, this theory of *virtù*, which governs the current destiny of Italy, but knew its finest historical hour in Rome, allows Machiavelli to search in Rome and its history for the exemplary historical *rehearsal* of those laws of political practice to be observed to ensure the triumph of Italian unity.

I thereby come to the *third example*: precisely Rome and, more generally, antiquity and the ancients. In the preface to Book I of the *Discourses*, Machiavelli waxes indignant over a flagrant contradiction. Rome is admired in everything: an infinite value is attached to the least fragment of statue with which a house is adorned, and its example is commended to artists. In literature, the arts, jurisprudence, and even medicine ('[no]thing other than the experiments performed by the doctors of antiquity upon which today's doctors and their diagnoses rely'[27]), Rome is admired and imitated. In everything – save politics:

> [I]n organizing republics, maintaining states, governing kingdoms, in instituting a militia and administering a war, in executing legal decisions among subjects, and in expanding an empire, no prince, republic, military leader, or citizen can be found who has recourse to the *examples* of the ancients.[28]

In this sentence we can begin to take the measure of Machiavelli's precise relationship to antiquity and Rome. Far from subscribing to the religious, moral, philosophical, or aesthetic myth fostered by humanism in respect of the ancients and Rome, to the *universal* ideological celebration of antiquity, Machiavelli vehemently denounces the *discrimination* imposed on it by its official eulogists and priests. He declares that his own antiquity is precisely the one sacrificed, forgotten, repressed: the antiquity of *politics*. Not the antiquity of philosophical theories of politics, but that of the concrete history and practice of politics. This is the antiquity he rescues from oblivion with passion, in denouncing the ideological contradiction of his time. Celebrated in the guise of fine art and literature, practised in jurisprudence and medicine, antiquity is spurned in politics. Machiavelli believes that this contradiction is not an inconsistency: on the contrary, he considers it a *consequence*. In fact, there is an immediate, direct relationship between the contempt of rulers, republics, captains and citizens for antiquity, when *virtù* was visibly realized, and their own practice or customs. If they have contempt for antiquity, it is because their practice is *contemptible*. Thus, it is from the viewpoint of a wholly positive and affirmative[29] political practice that Machiavelli relates to antiquity, proceeding directly to that dimension of it sacrificed in its moral and aesthetic celebration in the service of pathetic rulers: politics.

Here again, we witness the same effect of reliance and distantiation, or determinate 'negation', being produced. To constitute his experimental theory of history and politics, Machiavelli has granted himself the right to make comparisons between past and present events and conjunctures. He has done so through his thesis of the immutable order of things and men. Therewith he has been authorized to speak of the ancients. It is a universal right. But the antiquity he invokes is not universal; it is the antiquity *of which no one speaks*. In order to be able to resort to the latter, he grants himself the former and refuses it in one and the same movement. This negation produces the determination: namely, political antiquity, the antiquity of political practice – the only one that could be located in a relationship of theoretical comparison with the political present, to facilitate comprehension of the present, definition of the political objective, and political means of action. There now begins a constant to-ing and fro-ing between past and present, an interminable comparison (in the sense in which a psychoanalysis is interminable: like political action, it is never finished, but always to be resumed if one wishes it to endure). A comparison between antiquity, especially Rome – centre of centres of the past, *the example par excellence of the duration of a state* – and the present day, especially Italy – centre of centres of political *misery*, of which it could be said, as the young Marx was to say of Germany in 1842, that it has forgotten what history is 'because no history happens there' – and France or Spain, which have succeeded in building states that endure because they are national states. Just as Machiavelli does not apply a general theory of history to particular concrete cases, so he does not apply antiquity to the present. Just as the general theory of history intervenes solely on condition of being determined by a series of 'negations' that have meaning only as a function of the central political problem, so too antiquity intervenes only under the determination of Rome, in order to illuminate the centre of everything – the political *vacuum* of Italy – and the task of filling it.

Here the alleged difference between *The Prince* and the *Discourses* must be addressed. The conclusion Rousseau derived from this opposition will be recalled: Machiavelli is a crypto-republican who, in *The Prince*, gives the people lessons in republicanism, while feigning to instruct the Prince in tyranny. This means that, literally speaking, Machiavelli is tyrannical or monarchist in *The Prince*, but only so as to put rulers off the scent while instructing the people, whose side he openly takes only in the *Discourses on Livy*, where Machiavelli displays his true republican sentiments. This thesis is obviously false. It is true that in the first sentence of Chapter II of *The Prince*, beginning his examination of the different types of principality, Machiavelli writes: 'I shall not discuss republics, because I have previously treated them at length.'[30] There are two types of principality of which he says nothing, or virtually nothing: republics and ecclesiastical states. This is because he expects nothing from either of them as regards his political project. If he omits to mention them, it is because they have nothing to teach history. No one has seriously queried the significance of this silence: it is not a republic that will be capable of fashioning the Italian national state (we shall see why). But by this silence he refers his readers to the *Discourses*, where he talks at great length of republics. But in what sense?

It would take too long to embark upon a detailed discussion here. As an indication, I shall make do with citing the judgement of Barincou, who edited Machiavelli's texts for the Pléiade edition. He writes of the '*Discourses on Livy* that Machiavelli had begun to write for use in a republic and which he abandoned, recasting their substance and reducing it to a kind of monarchistic breviary'.[31] Let us clarify this judgement. The republic of all republics is Rome, centre of all antiquity. But Rome affords the singular peculiarity *of being a republic founded by kings*,[32] which would never have been what it was without them.

This puts us on the track. Hitherto we had been able to establish a correlation between the state that endures, the (monarchical) combination of powers, and *virtù*. We now see a new term emerge: that of the *beginning*, the *foundation*. The monarchy–republic opposition supposedly illustrated by the contrast between *The Prince* and the *Discourses* falls. What concerns Machiavelli is not this oversimplified typology and its contrasting terms. What interests him is the foundation and beginning of a durable state which, once founded by a Prince, will prove durable as a result of a 'composite' government. Machiavelli's centre of interest in antiquity, which is going to organize all his analyses – that is to say, govern all the questions he poses – is then irresistibly fixed. *This centre is Rome, a state that endured. The centre of Rome resides in its beginnings. The beginning of this republic was to have been a monarchy*, endowing Rome with a government conducive to the state's durability – *a composite government that persisted under the guise of the republic.* The extent to which this antiquity was totally foreign to that of the contemporary humanists is evident, as is the meaning of his exercise in comparative experience for Machiavelli. Antiquity is the antiquity of states, politics and political practice. This state and politics are Rome. But Rome is not a state among others, a republic alongside monarchies or tyrannies, particular features of which could be compared. Rome is par excellence *the observable objective experience of the foundation of a state that endured*, and endured for specific reasons pertaining on the one hand to its foundation by *kings*, and on the other to the *laws* given it by these rulers. Rome is thus the formulation of a problem resolved: the very problem of Italy for Machiavelli. At the heart of Machiavelli's reflection and discourse we here once again encounter the same to-ing and fro-ing between past and present, general theory and concrete problem; between general considerations, political problem, and concrete political practice. Machiavelli's antiquity has the same relationship with the present as his theory of history has with the political problem he poses, which is posed by the present conjuncture, and dictates adoption of the viewpoint of political practice.

In this respect, Machiavelli's treatment of antiquity is interesting on another account. It has enabled us to grasp Machiavelli's originality; it is now going to reveal his limits. But even his limits are original.

I shall go to the crux of the matter in a few words. If the novel relations to theory and antiquity that we have just analysed are original and positively fertile, it remains the case that they are not devoid of a certain illusion: the *utopian* illusion. If it is true that every utopia scans the past for the guarantee and shape of the future, Machiavelli, who seeks the future solution to Italy's political problem in Rome, does not escape the illusion of utopia.

The question that must then be posed is this: *in what* does this illusion consist? A question that merges with another question: why did Machiavelli *need* this illusion?

We are bound to associate these two questions with the answer given them by Marx in the opening pages of *The Eighteenth Brumaire*, precisely in connection with a revolutionary political problem – that of the French Revolution – and recourse to Rome. Marx contrasts the new revolution announced by the *Communist Manifesto* with the French Revolution. Unlike the French Revolution, it has no need of utopia; it no longer needs to seek its future in the past. Why? Marx writes:

> The social revolution of the nineteenth century can only create its poetry from the future, not from the past. It cannot begin its own work until it has sloughed off all its superstitious regard for the past. Earlier revolutions have needed world-historical reminiscences to deaden their awareness of their own content.[33]

Take the French Revolution, for example:

> Camille Desmoulins, Danton, Robespierre, Saint-Just and Napoleon, the heroes of the old French Revolution, as well as its parties and masses, accomplished the task of their epoch, which was the emancipation and establishment of modern *bourgeois* society, in *Roman costume* and with *Roman slogans*. . . . And its gladiators found in the stern classical *traditions* of the Roman republic, the *ideals, art forms* and *illusions* they needed in order to hide from themselves the *limited bourgeois content* of their struggles and to maintain their enthusiasm at the high level appropriate to great historical tragedy.[34]

In these remarks (where he also refers to Cromwell), Marx states what he regards as the law, if not of every revolution, at least of bourgeois revolution: bourgeois revolution always advances backwards, breaking into the future with its eyes turned to the past. Or rather, it advances into the future only preceded by the past. It involves an illusion, but a necessary illusion. Why necessary? Because without these mythical examples of the Roman accomplishment of liberty, equality and fraternity, without the ideology of Roman political virtue, the leaders and protagonists of the bourgeois revolution would not have been able to mobilize the masses, *would not have been able to mobilize themselves*, to carry out the revolution and bring it to completion. If they required the past, it is because they needed its illusion: they needed the *excess* of the past relative to the present, in order to disguise the *narrowness* of the *actual content* of the bourgeois revolution. They needed to believe that they were embarking on the conquest of liberty, equality and fraternity, were fighting and dying for these ideals, when bourgeois revolution could *only* liberate men from feudal relations of exploitation, and then solely so as to subject them to bourgeois–capitalist relations of exploitation: formal liberty, but substantive inequality, in a new mode of exploitation.

I leave to one side the mechanism of this compensation and illusion, enigmatic in *The Eighteenth Brumaire*. In a word, we shall say that it consists entirely in the specific contradiction of the French Revolution, and bourgeois revolution in general: namely, that it is a struggle for state power *betweeen two equally exploitative classes*, feudal aristocracy and bourgeoisie. In this struggle the urban and rural exploited classes (Mathiez's 'Fourth Estate'[35]) are *mobilized* under a utopian ideology in the service of the class struggle of the new exploiting class, the bourgeoisie. Such mobilization is possible because this new class already possesses its social and material basis of exploitation in the old society in which it has developed. The utopia signalled by Marx, then, is nothing other than the form in which the bourgeoisie mobilizes its own exploited (and mobilizes itself) in pursuit of its political objectives: the capture of state power. It is nothing but the necessary effect of the disjuncture of the class struggle of the exploited, and its subordination to the struggle pitting two exploiting classes against one another. The Roman utopia of the popular revolutionaries compensates for this disjuncture.

I now pose the question: is this the type of utopia we are dealing with in Machiavelli? Does Machiavelli's Rome play the same utopian role that Rome played for the revolutionaries of 1789–93? Does the Roman ideology represent the same necessary illusion, intended to disguise the limited content of a first form of bourgeois revolution?

In fact, it involves a radically different form. To be convinced, it is enough to note that Rome in no way provides Machiavelli with what it supplied to the revolutionaries of 1789 – namely, 'the *language*, the *passions* and the *illusions*' of a *moral* ideology.[36] What – following Rousseau – the revolutionaries seek in Rome is examples of political virtue, hatred of tyranny, love of liberty, equality and fatherland, incorruptibility, the sense of duty: let us say, moral *virtues*, moral forms of conduct in respect of politics and, therewith, a moral ideology of politics. In these two regards, Machiavelli is at the antipodes of this ideology. What he seeks in Rome is not the elements of a moral ideology, but quite the opposite: proof, among other things, of the need to subordinate morality to politics. He seeks not *virtue*, but *virtù*, which has nothing moral about it, for it exclusively designates the exceptional political ability and intellectual *power* of the Prince.[37]

In this respect, it could be said that Machiavelli, while speaking of Rome, in a certain way anticipates the manifesto of the nineteenth-century revolution – the social revolution – which no longer needs to invoke an imaginary Rome. By this we mean that it no longer needs, as Marx puts it, to resort to the past to think its future; to be more precise, it no longer requires, in Marx's words, 'the phrase [that] transcend[s] the content';[38] to be more precise still, it no longer needs to imagine its concrete political objectives in the shape of a *moral* ideology borrowed from a myth of the past. And this is because, in taking his untrodden path, Machiavelli has definitively broken with the illusions of moral ideology. He treats Rome as a politician, compares Rome with France and Spain, and presents his 'case' – the *guarantee* of the potential existence of a state that endures, and the theory of its conditions of existence – solely as proof that his theory of the aleatory invariant is *true*.[39]

So Machiavelli's utopianism does not consist in resort to Rome as the prop for a moral ideology that is required in the present. It consists in recourse to Rome as *guarantee* or *rehearsal* for a *necessary* task, whose concrete conditions of possibility are, however, *impossible* to define. Rome ensures and guarantees the link between this necessity and this impossibility. Accordingly, the discrepancy that makes it a utopia is a discrepancy not between the narrowness of the current sociopolitical content and the necessary universal illusion of moral ideology, but between a *necessary* political task and its conditions of realization, which are possible and conceivable, and yet at the same time *impossible* and *inconceivable*, because aleatory.[40] With this we re-encounter the two previous viewpoints – that of the Prince and that of the people – in a certain fashion. But I do not want to anticipate. I would simply say that Machiavelli's utopia is quite specific, distinguished from every other utopia by the following characteristic: it is not an ideological utopia; nor is it *for the most part* a political utopia. It is a *theoretical* utopia, by which we mean that it occurs, and produces its effects, *in theory*. Indeed, it merges with Machiavelli's endeavour to think the conditions of possibility of an impossible task, to think the unthinkable. I deliberately say *to think*, and not to imagine, dream, or hit upon ideal solutions. As we shall see, it is because he faced up to the effort of thinking the unthinkable as such that Machiavelli found himself engaged in forms of thought without any precedent.

The Theory of the 'New Prince'

Now that we have some acquaintance with Machiavelli's *mode* of thinking and its effects, we can get to the heart of his theory, which might be called a theory of the 'New Prince'.

We know what the problem posed by Machiavelli is: the constitution of Italian national unity. We are dealing not with an interpretation – Gramsci's, largely adopted from De Sanctis[1] – but with a stance that Machiavelli makes explicit. He does so in several places in *The Prince* and the *Discourses* – for example, in Book I, Chapter 12 of the *Discourses*, in connection with condemnation of the Roman Catholic Church's politics:

> [T]he church has kept and still keeps this land divided, and truly, *no land is ever united or happy unless it comes completely under the obedience of a single republic or a single prince*, as has occurred in France and Spain. The reason why Italy is not in that same condition and why it . . . does not have either a single republic or a single prince to govern it lies solely with the church, because although the church has its place of residence in Italy and has held temporal power there, it has not been so powerful nor has it possessed enough skill to be able to occupy the remaining parts of Italy and make itself ruler of this country. . . .[2]

In Chapter XXVI of *The Prince*, Machiavelli exhorts Lorenzo de' Medici 'to liberate Italy from the barbarian yoke'. To liberate Italy is to deliver the nation *of the Italians*, to make a nation of Italy under a *new Prince*. And the *conjuncture* comes in straight away: Italy is there for the taking. Why? Because in Italy, 'there is matter that provides an opportunity for a far-seeing and able man to mould it into a form that will bring honour to him and benefit all its inhabitants'.[3] The *form* will be a *New Principality* under a New Prince, who unifies the country not under a tyrant, but under a king governing by laws. The *matter* is the condition of Italy at 'the present time' – in other words, a conjuncture dominated by three characteristics.

The first is the extreme misery of Italy, which plumbs the depths of historical nullity, hence emptiness:[4]

> [I]n order for the valour and worth of an Italian spirit to be recognised, Italy had to be reduced to the *desperate straits* in which it now finds itself: more enslaved than the Hebrews, more oppressed than the Persians, more scattered than the Athenians, without an acknowledged leader, and without order or stability, beaten, despoiled, lacerated, overrun, in short, utterly devastated.[5]

It is as if the extremity of these ills had rendered Italy *formless*, and hence ready – more so than an already formed country – to be shaped by a new sculptor. The calamities of its history have made Italy like a shapeless, brute matter that the Prince will be able to mould more readily, like a blank sheet on which the New Prince can write anything.

The second characteristic is that this political *vacuum* is simply an immense aspiration to political *being* – witness the expectation and general consensus, 'how ready and willing' Italy is:

> The opportunity to provide Italy with a liberator, then, after such a long time, must not be missed. I have no doubt at all that he would be received with great affection in all those regions that have been inundated by the foreign invasions, as well as with a great thirst for revenge, with resolute fidelity, with devotion and with tears of gratitude. What gate would be closed to him? What people would fail to obey him? What envious hostility would work against him? What Italian would deny him homage?[6]

If the matter is brute and the sheet blank, the popular consensus is already completely behind the New Prince, who will unify Italy, suppress its divisions, and prevent the intervention of other, *foreign* states. Indeed, a new nation can be engendered only in military struggle against already constituted foreign nations.

The third characteristic is that, in still more precise guise, 'there is no lack of matter to shape into any form'[7] – not the brute political matter, but another determinate matter, an already fashioned raw material: the *virtù* of *individual* Italians. The proof? The valour of the Italians, who 'in duels and combats between several men ... are superior in strength, skill and resourcefulness'. Yet 'when it comes to fighting in armies, they do not distinguish themselves. And all this stems from the weakness of the leaders.'[8] In other words, Italians are individually endowed with *virtù*; they are lacking only in military *virtù*, which derives from leaders, and political *virtù*, which issues from the Prince.

To sum up the given elements of the conjuncture: Italian matter awaits only an appropriate form to unify the nation. The extreme wretchedness and destitution of Italy, the expectation and consensus of its peoples, the *virtù* of its individuals: here is the matter. Political nullity, individual wealth – everything is set for the intervention of the *liberator* Prince (a formula in the air since Dante: the deliverer, 'the hound'[9]).

So the political objective is quite openly avowed and clear. In these circumstances it seems as if the answer should be equally simple and evident. Italy must be unified under an *existing* ruler; and this is Machiavelli's move at the end of *The Prince*, when he addresses Lorenzo de' Medici. However, this solution encounters a minor obstacle: the fact that in *The Prince*, and as an aside in the *Discourses*, Machiavelli never stops insisting on the twin theme of the New Prince and the New Principality – not only on each of the individual terms, but on the *pair* of them, as if he intended to signal something essential, an essential *difficulty* that resonates like a leitmotiv. 'Nobody should be surprised if, in discussing completely new principalities, both as regards the ruler and the type of government, I shall cite remarkable men as forbears.'[10] This is because it is necessary to 'aim at a much higher point ... to be able to strike [the] target'.[11] Why? Because 'it is in new principalities that there are real difficulties'.[12] Let us get to the bottom of the difficulty. It consists in the fact that for Machiavelli there is no solution other than this *very difficulty*. On closer inspection, it is no accident if Machiavelli describes Italy as plumbing the depths of political nullity: the matter does indeed exist there – namely, individual *virtù* and popular consent – but not, ultimately, any *form* genuinely primed for the political task of national unity. Ultimately, this form must be completely new: a new Prince and a new Principality. Why *ultimately*?

To clarify what follows, I shall anticipate and immediately indicate that Machiavelli finds himself in a situation that obliges him to reason *in ultimate terms*, to think at the limits of the possible in order to think about the real. Machiavelli's insistence on referring to a New Prince and a New Principality is located in this extreme position, where he is condemned to thinking the possible at the boundary of the impossible. We shall see the theoretical consequences.

But in order to demonstrate the importance and meaning of the theme of novelty in detail, I am going to conduct an analysis in two stages; and so that I myself face up to the greatest difficulty, I shall begin with a foray into the *Discourses*, before going into *The Prince*.

If Book I of the *Discourses* is read from this standpoint, their compatibility with *The Prince* is evident. In fact, what Machiavelli is seeking to define in the *Discourses*, in an ancient history focused on Rome and constantly paralleled with contemporary history, is theoretical *arguments* for the theses set out in *The Prince*.

Accordingly, Chapter 1 is devoted to 'What the beginnings of cities have always been, and what the beginnings of Rome were like'. Machiavelli thus straight away commences with his essential theme: the beginnings – that is to say, the foundation – of a state. But we are immediately going to witness the intervention of a form of reasoning peculiar to him – the dilemma – and its result: the exclusion of one term in favour of another, the closure of one space inducing the opening of another. Machiavelli's immediate dilemma is revealing. He writes: 'men act either out of necessity or by choice, and . . . ability is greater where choice has less authority'.[13] Whence the conclusion: cities and states should be founded on barren sites – the void once again;[14] virtue (moral virtue: not *virtù*) would prevail there, and discord would be unknown. An example is Ragusa. But the hypothesis is advanced only to be rejected. Such a state would be poor and weak, incapable of *defending itself* and *expanding*. Men 'must . . . situate themselves in the most fertile regions, where . . . the richness of the site allows them to expand'.[15] In the most fertile sites, however, men will be condemned to vice. No matter: laws will have to be imposed to compel them, especially in their capacity as soldiers, to *virtù*. In this brief theoretical exchange with which the *Discourses* open, things are put in place at once. The utopia of an ideal city, uncultivated and pure, virtuous in the moral sense, is ruled out *once and for all*, since it does not correspond to the conditions on which Machiavelli has his sights: *self-defence and expansion*. Once and for all, men must be taken as they are: 'it is necessary for anyone who organizes a republic . . . to take for granted that all men are evil'.[16] Politically, one must ignore their moral qualities, their virtue, and impose *laws* on them, so as to induce something quite distinct from moral virtue: military and political *virtù*.

Laws are precisely what is in question in Chapter 2: 'How many kinds of republics there are, and what kind the Roman republic was'. Once again, Machiavelli rules out one hypothesis from the outset:

> I wish to set aside an examination of those cities that had their beginnings while subject to others, and I shall speak of those cities that had their beginnings far removed from any kind of external servitude and were immediately governed by their *own laws either* as republics *or* as principalities. . . .[17]

We can appreciate the sense in which Machiavelli speaks of republics in the *Discourses*. The chapter title refers exclusively to republics, including Rome. The text – and this is constantly the case in the *Discourses* – concerns either republics or principalities, treated on a par. Thus, what matters to Machiavelli is not the distinction between them, but what they have in common historically. And this common characteristic, this invariant,[18] is an absolute prerequisite: from the perspective of a New Principality conducive to Italian unification, it is the rejection of any hypothesis of foreign domination, and the *independence* of the origin and character of the laws, which must be *peculiar* to the new state. Just beneath the surface we can read the thesis underpinning this analysis: the new state must owe its beginnings exclusively to itself; it must owe its laws solely to itself. To speak more plainly: the state that is to unify the Italian nation cannot be a foreign state; it must be a national state. There follows the theory of the cycle of history; the comparative analysis of Sparta, Athens, and finally Rome; the theme of the *duration* of the state;

and the theme of 'composite government' on the Roman model – that is to say, a state founded by kings, which preserved the monarchical mould when it became a republic. The theory of the conditions for the foundation and duration of the new state are thus sketched (as an aside) in connection with an antiquity that is extremely present and modern.

In Chapters 3 and 4 we progress further, discovering the reason for this 'composite government' and its distinctive feature: *laws*. On this theme Machiavelli returns to the thesis underpinning his rejection of the utopia of a poor and virtuous city: 'men never do good except out of necessity'.[19] By *'out of necessity'* we may understand either the dominion of *fear*, or the constraint of laws:

> Hence, it is said that hunger and poverty make men industrious and laws make them good, and where something works well by itself without the law, the law is unnecessary, but when that good custom is lacking, the law is immediately necessary.[20]

Thus, in Rome, for example, 'after the Tarquins were gone, fear of whom had kept the nobility in check, it was necessary to consider a new institution that would produce the same effect [as] the Tarquins'. This new institution was the creation of tribunes, who could 'act as intermediaries between the plebeians and the senate and . . . curb the insolence of the nobles'.[21] With this we enter into the 'dialectic' of laws.[22] Bearing in mind that the existence of laws is indispensable to the form of 'composite government' that is Machiavelli's political objective, and knowing that he lauds France nearly as much as Rome, because it has a form of government wherein the king rules through *laws*, we soon suspect, after what has just been said of the Tarquins, that laws are not *the general form* of political constraint. We discover that there is another form – fear – and even that laws, far from leading to the disappearance of fear, simply displace it: after the Tarquins, it is laws that curb the nobles. An element of fear is thus involved in laws, once again excluding the myth of a purely moral city. The truth of laws, in effect, appears as a *function* of the conflicts between antagonistic social groups in the state, sometimes called nobles and people by Machiavelli, sometimes 'opposing humours', and sometimes *classes*. This is the celebrated theory of the two 'humours': 'there is nothing that makes a

republic so stable and steady as organizing it in such a way that
... those humours that agitate the republic [have] a means of
release that is instituted by the laws'.[23] In Book I, Chapter 4 of
the *Discourses*, it is said that 'in every republic there are two
different tendencies, that of the people and that of the upper
class, and ... all of the laws which are passed in favour of liberty
are born from the rift between the two'.[24] Whence the thesis,
which goes against the current of prevalent opinion, that 'good
laws [arise from] those disturbances that many people thought-
lessly condemn'.[25] Since, in the examples cited, these disturbances issue from the people, who rebel against the nobles, there
is no doubt that Machiavelli considers laws in their relationship
with the class struggle from a double angle. In their *outcome*,
they stabilize the balance of forces between classes and then
operate (as he puts it) as an 'intermediary', engendering 'liberty'.
But in their 'cause', they prioritize the people, whose 'disturbances' result in the conquest of laws. In his theory of the class
struggle as the origin of the laws that limit it, Machiavelli adopts
the viewpoint of the people.

This emerges from Chapter IX of *The Prince* and Book I,
Chapter 16 of the *Discourses*. In *The Prince* Machiavelli writes:
'these two classes [nobles and people] are found in every city.
And this situation arises because the people do not want to be
dominated or oppressed by the nobles, and the nobles want to
dominate and oppress the people.'[26] And in the *Discourses* we
read:

> [A] small part of the people wishes to be free in order to command,
> but all the others, who are countless, desire liberty in order to live in
> safety.... [they] can be easily satisfied by establishing institutions
> and passing laws which provide for both the prince's personal power
> and the public safety.... An example of this is the Kingdom of
> France, which lives in security for no other reason than the fact that
> its kings are constrained by countless laws which also provide for
> the security of all its people.[27]

But this last sentence discloses a third personage, over and above
the class struggle: the king. Machiavelli's thesis is that in the
conflict between nobility and people, the king takes the people's
side by decreeing laws. This is one of the themes of Chapter IX
of *The Prince: it is better to be the people's ruler than the nobles'*:

[T]he nobles cannot be satisfied if a ruler acts honourably, without injuring others. But the people can be thus satisfied, because their aims are more honourable than those of the nobles: for the latter want only to oppress, and the former only to avoid being oppressed.[28]

And similarly, Book I, Chapter 5 of the *Discourses* (to which I shall return) explains that liberty is better entrusted to the people than to the nobility, because the latter (nobility) have 'a strong desire to dominate', whereas the former (people) 'only . . . desire not to be dominated, and, as a consequence, [possess] a stronger will to live in liberty'.[29] Machiavelli's partisanship is clear: government by a Prince 'constrained by countless laws' – or, as he puts it elsewhere, by a 'system of laws'[30] – is government by a Prince who takes the people's side in their struggle with the nobles.

To take this side is to run the risk of disturbances, as in Rome. Can they be avoided, asks Machiavelli in the title of Book I, Chapter 6 of the *Discourses*? Might it have been 'possible to organize a government that could do away with the enmities between the people and the Senate'? This brief chapter is a gem of comparative demonstration, and it ends with a dilemma: 'To examine this matter,' Machiavelli writes, 'it is necessary to refer to those republics which, without such enmities and disturbances, remained free for a long period of time and to see what kind of government they possessed and whether it could have been introduced in Rome.'[31] The comparative table comprises Sparta (a 'republic'!) and Venice – hence an ancient and a modern example. At stake is the question of Rome: could it have avoided conflict beween nobles and plebeians? Everything is in place for a variegated comparison and theoretical reduction. And here are the results. Machiavelli observes that if Venice has proved capable of avoiding conflicts, it is by making all citizens of Venetian origin gentlemen who make laws in councils, while allowing foreigners to come and live in the city; consequently, there was never an intolerable gulf between nobles and the rest. Machiavelli notes that if Sparta avoided conflicts, it was because foreigners were excluded and there were practically no nobles interposed between monarch and people. He concludes:

Hence in taking into consideration all these things, one sees that Rome's legislators had to do one of two things if they wanted Rome to remain as peaceful as the two republics mentioned above: either they could avoid using the plebeians in warfare, as the Venetians did, or they could avoid giving open access to foreigners, as the Spartans did.[32]

The Romans, however, 'did both the one and the other: this gave the plebeians strength and an increase in their numbers, as well as countless opportunities to create disturbances'.[33] For the republic to have been more peaceful, it would have had to be *weaker*. But in that event, 'it would have cut itself off from the path to realizing the greatness it attained, so that, had Rome wished to eliminate the causes of her disturbances, she would also have eliminated the causes for her expansion'.[34]

A curious comparative method! Machiavelli extracts two sorts of conditions from Venice and Sparta; and he rejects them in the Roman case. Why? Because they are incompatible with Rome's destiny. The Venetian and Spartan conditions are conditions for weak states, by which is understood states incapable of *expanding*. Here there are two appreciable, decisive points: using the plebeians in warfare and being able to assimilate foreigners – in other words, increasing the people's strength. Everything thus stems from the people: either increase their numbers and give them arms, in which case you become strong; or limit and disarm them, in which case you remain weak. Here is the dilemma. There are two utterly distinct, *incompatible types of state*: those that subsist in weakness; and those strong enough and so constructed that they *expand*. And here is the text's turning point, where the tone changes. Machiavelli's impeccably objective, objectivist, and serene comparison ends with a direct address: 'Consequently, if you wish to create a numerous and well-armed people, in order to build a great empire, you create it with such qualities that you cannot then manage it as you wish.'[35] You will have disturbances; but you will succeed in *expanding*. Otherwise, you will have a people free of disturbances, but you will not be able to expand and will be at the mercy of anyone who happens by. We must choose what we want: as Machiavelli says, 'we must consider where the fewest drawbacks lie and take that as the best alternative, because an option that is completely clear

and completely without uncertainty cannot ever be found'.[36]
Note carefully: 'the fewest drawbacks' *not in the abstract, but*
solely in respect of the political objective being pursued.

'If', Machiavelli writes shortly afterwards, 'anyone wishes . . .
to organize an entirely new republic, he should examine whether
he would like it to expand in size and power like Rome, or to
remain within narrow limits. In the first case, it is necessary to
organize it like Rome.'[37] In other words, it is necessary to pay the
price of 'disturbances and widespread disagreements' – of *class
struggle* between people and nobility – to achieve the equivalent
of Roman greatness, which acts as a paradigm of the national
state. For Machiavelli the choice has been made, and made
between the two terms of the alternative, for *there is no middle way*:

> [I]t is necessary to follow the political organization of Rome and not
> that of other republics, because *I cannot believe that it is possible to find
> a middle way between the one alternative and the other,* and it is necessary
> to tolerate those enmities that arose between the people and the
> senate, taking them as a disadvantage necessary to attain Roman
> greatness.[38]

Machiavelli does not say that class struggle is the motor of
history; he does say that class struggle is necessary, indispensable to the development of any state that wants to *expand* and
endure while it expands – expand, that is to say, grow to become
the state of the nation. If we have borne in mind Machiavelli's
assertion that the Prince must take the side of the people, not the
nobility, in this struggle, all these propositions converge on a
thesis involving a very clear stance: the new state must be a state
that lasts; for that, it must be equipped with laws expressing the
balance of forces in the class struggle between nobles and people;
in this struggle the Prince must rely on the people; the class
struggle is indispensable to impart to the state not only *duration*,
but also the capacity to expand, that is to say, become a national
state.

This is what we can read in the first six chapters of Book I of
the *Discourses*. If anyone then wants to argue that what is
involved is a profession of republican faith, words – I mean
propositions and their organization – mean nothing. Here, too,
is how Machiavelli proceeds in his 'comparisons' between past
and present, between the different cases: all the 'laws' he derives

from them are alternatives; that is to say, they do nothing but connect some objective conditions and their effects with some potential options. In his comparisons Machiavelli is simply looking for *alternative conditions for the attainment of his political objective*.

I pass over Chapters 7 and 8, dealing with indictments and accusations, which are simply variations on the theme of laws in relation to the people, and come to Chapter 9, which is decisive when it is paired with Chapter 10. Chapter 9 is entitled: 'That a man must be alone if he wishes to organize a new republic or completely to reform its ancient institutions'; and Chapter 10: 'The founders of a republic or a kingdom [*sic*] deserve as much praise as those who found a tyranny deserve blame'. Under the rubric of 'republics', more monarchies than republics feature in these chapters! And the question is settled right away. That is to say, a hypothesis is once again excluded and an option affirmed: tyranny is condemned in radical terms. The symbol of tyranny is Caesar – not Cesare Borgia, but the Roman Caesar – proving that Rome is not always in Rome, and that even inside Rome Machiavelli can contrast one Rome with another: 'Caesar is all the more detestable, just like the man who is to be blamed more for committing an evil deed than for wishing to do so.'[39] What is the evil deed committed by Caesar? – when we know that Machiavelli has just excused the crime of Romulus, saying:

[N]or will a wise mind ever reproach anyone for an illegal action that he might have undertaken to organize a kingdom or to constitute a republic. It is truly appropriate that while the act accuses him, the result excuses him, and when the result is good, like that of Romulus, it will always excuse him, because one should reproach a man who is violent in order to ruin things, not one who is so in order to set them aright.[40]

When we appreciate this, we understand that *not every end* justifies 'illegal' means; and that Caesar's goal was unforgivable because he committed the unpardonable crime of establishing tyranny in Rome. This end has been judged on its *results*, whose dreadful inventory is drawn up by Machiavelli at the conclusion of Chapter 10. By contrast, we understand that Romulus' end was good so long as we 'consider the goal which led [him] to commit such a homicide' – that of his brother and his companion. This goal was to be *alone*, to remain alone on the stage. Why? So as to organize the republic (or kingdom!).

This thesis is fundamental in Machiavelli: that 'it is necessary to be *alone* to found a new republic or completely reform it'. The foundation of a state, the beginnings of a state, or the complete reformation that is also an absolute (re)commencement in the course of history – in short, *every absolute beginning requires the absolute solitude of the reformer or founder*. The Prince's solitude is the precise correlate of the *vacuum* of the conjuncture.[41] '[I]t is necessary for a *single* man to be the one who gives it shape, and from whose mind any such organization derives.'[42] And Machiavelli proceeds to invoke countless potential examples, including Moses, Lycurgus, Solon and others, 'who were able to create *laws* for the common good, because they had assumed for themselves *sole authority*', concentrating *all* authority in themselves.[43] The solitude of the state's founder is dictated by the exceptional conditions of his enterprise, which demands that he should possess undivided powers: '[T]he many are not capable of instituting anything, being unable to recognize its goodness, because of the diversity of opinions that exist among them'.[44] In order to derive a state from nothing, the founder must be alone; that is to say, be everything: omnipotent – omnipotent before the *vacuum* of the conjuncture and its aleatory future.[45]

He would, however, be nothing more than a tyrant were he to wield this total power arbitrarily. He is the founder of a state (worthy of the name) only if he gives it laws and, through these laws, resigns his exclusive powers and emerges from his solitude: 'although one man alone is capable of instituting a government, what he has instituted will not long endure if it rests upon the shoulders of a single man, but it endures when it remains a matter of concern to many and when it is the task of many to maintain it'.[46] Machiavelli's thesis therewith takes more precise shape. I recall that he has in mind an absolute object of reference – *the new state* – and that in the *Discourses* he seeks to define the conditions of its advent via historical comparisons. We are at the point where he reaches a decisive conclusion, distinguishing *two moments* in the constitution of a state. (1) The first moment is that of the absolute *beginning*, which is necessarily the deed of one man alone, 'a single individual'. But this moment is itself unstable, for ultimately it can as readily tip over into tyranny as into an authentic state. Whence (2) the second moment, that of *duration*, which can be ensured only by a double process: the settlement of laws and emergence from solitude – that is to say, the end of the absolute power of a single individual. Now we know that laws are linked to the existence of contending classes, and that they above all establish recognition of the people. Duration obtains, then, exclusively through laws, by which the Prince can 'take root' in his people.

Two principal metaphors correspond to these two moments. To the first moment corresponds the metaphor of foundation, the founder, the edifice: this is the abstract, formal moment of beginnings, when the founder lays the foundation of the edifice in designing its organization; in *decreeing*, only when he decrees them, laws – it is on this account that he can be a lawgiver. To the second moment corresponds the metaphor of taking root: this is the concrete, organic moment either of the penetration of the laws thus decreed into the antagonistic social classes, or of the production of laws by popular struggle against the nobles. This rooting of the Prince's power in the people by the mechanism of laws is the absolute condition for the state's *duration* and *power* – that is to say, its capacity to *expand*.

So long as their distinctiveness is borne in mind, these two moments can help us to think the difference between *The Prince* and the *Discourses* – in other words, their non-difference, their profound unity.

If in *The Prince* emphasis is put on the first moment – absolute power, an absolute monarchy – this is because it is the absolute form of the beginning of the state. If in the *Discourses* emphasis is put on what have been called republics, but which (as Machiavelli himself constantly reiterates) are just as much principalities – especially Rome, that republic founded by kings who preserved the royal mould while changing their titles – it is because Machiavelli is predominantly studying the *second moment* there: the moment of the forms which permit state power to take root in the people, via the intermediary of laws, and render the state capable of both *enduring* and *expanding*, thus of surmounting the test of time and space. In the aftermath of the founding moment, stress is no longer placed on absolute power, but on composite government, laws, and the people. Very schematically, let us say that a state can be founded only by a single individual, hence by a king (in this regard Machiavelli is strictly monarchist); but that the same state can endure in time and expand in space only if it transforms its constitution to institutionalize the popular roots of power. This is what led the Encyclopaedists, Rousseau, Foscolo, and the ideologues of the *Risorgimento* to believe that Machiavelli was a republican, whereas his privileged example of a republic is Rome, which we know to be utterly distinct from a simple republic. Rome is the successful conversion of the absolutist form of the state's beginnings into the *durable* form of its legal – that is, popular – functioning under kings, whether they bear the title of consul (as in Rome) or king (as in France), who ensure its *expansion*.

The distinction between the two moments, and their specific conditions, is crucial, for it allows us to read *The Prince* and identify its particular object. I therefore halt examination of Book I of the *Discourses* at this precise point, to turn to *The Prince*.

Let us draw the lesson of this simple reading of Book I of the *Discourses*. My aim was first of all to show, to demonstrate, that the *Discourses* are not an utterly distinct text from *The Prince*; that Machiavelli does not have two faces; that, on the contrary, he has only one position. Next, my intention was to show, to demonstrate, that the *Discourses* do not discuss something different from *The Prince*: they discuss the *same thing*, and arrive at the same point, but via general comparisons whose function is to define the theoretical space of the object of *The Prince*, to allow us to situate that object with precision. To define this theoretical space is to define the general conditions of possibility for the historical *existence* – that is to say, the beginning and duration – of a state, via comparisons between ancient states, classical monarchies and republics. Without in any way prompting the texts, however, but simply by noting the way in which they work – that is to say, what they *exclude* simply by virtue of formulating what they *formulate*, the space they close by virtue of the space they open – we are obliged to observe that these general conditions for a state's historical existence are *defined* and *limited*: they are defined by the political problem posed by Machiavelli and the political objective this problem imposes.

Let us summarize the exclusions. The first is tyranny: one space has been closed. But to close down this space is to open up another. What? Tyranny is condemned on account of the

dreadful calamities accompanying it. Among them is the hardship suffered by the people. But this hardship discloses a reality:
tyranny is directed against the people, and it incites their hatred
and rebellion. Tyranny does not endure, for it cannot root itself
in the people; it cannot rely on their strength: it does not endure
and cannot expand.

Now let us assume governments that do endure, but in
conditions condemning them to organic weakness and preclud-
ing any expansion. Machiavelli excludes these, too, like the
ascetic utopia of the poor and virtuous city, or governments that
do not enhance the people's strength or are not in a condition to
arm them. For if such governments can endure in time, they are
at the mercy of a stronger rival, and they remain weak because
they are not in a condition to *expand*. This second exclusion
closes down a second space, but simultaneously opens up
another, intersecting with the same space that the exclusion of
tyranny opened up: the space of a state that endures and
constantly enhances its strength – that of the people – in order
to be capable of expanding. Meanwhile, the exclusion of tyranny
has also opened up a quite different space: that of laws, their
relation to the class struggle, and the need to accept this productive conflict if a state is to be both strong and capable of
expansion. By means of a methodical theoretical regression, the
ultimate question then emerges: the conditions of possibility for
the existence of a state thus defined. There, too, an exclusion
opens up another space to us: this state will be founded not by
many people, but by a single individual. And a final exclusion
delimits the new space straight away: if he wishes to found a
state that endures and grows strong, the one who is alone in
order to found it must emerge from the solitude of the founding
moment, and *'become many'*, precisely so as to root the state in
the people by means of laws and derive from them a popular,
that is – Machiavelli's ultimate objective – a national strength.

Now, there is nothing arbitrary about the distinction between
the two moments. Indeed, this distinction is nothing other than
a *statement* of the problem of *The Prince*. For the problem of *The
Prince* is *par excellence* the problem of the New Prince. It is the
problem of beginnings. To the question that has forever haunted
philosophy, and always will – with what should one *begin*? –
Machiavelli replies quite non-philosophically, but with theses

not lacking in philosophical resonance: one should begin with
the beginning. The beginning is ultimately nothing. And thus
are we plunged into the text of *The Prince* itself. It is necessary to
begin with a New Prince and a New Principality: that is to say,
literally and ultimately, with nothing – not 'nothingness', but
emptiness.[47]

We can now tackle *The Prince*. I am not going to offer a line-
by-line commentary; I should like to try to bring out its essential
features and theses.

If the problem of *The Prince* is that of beginnings, it seems
appropriate to do it the courtesy of beginning at the beginning,
its opening, and inquire what its function is.

The whole secret of *The Prince* lies in the way it is organized.
Now, this is outlined in the first chapter, which is entitled 'The
different kinds of principality and how they are acquired'. Thus
we have an impeccably general question, an inventory of kinds,
a *typology* apparently – not bearing on governments in general,
but solely on principalities governed by princes. Indeed, at the
beginning of Chapter II Machiavelli says: 'I shall not discuss
republics, because I have previously treated them at length.'[48]
Knowing how Machiavelli treats Rome, we appreciate how this
omission is provisionally to be construed. We shall see precisely
what it means later. But the question posed is decidedly curious,
because *two* questions are posed: how many different kinds of
principality are there (this is the typology)? *And* (contained in
the same question), how are they *acquired*? The chapter title alone
calls for two remarks. First, the typology announced in the first
part of the question – how many different kinds of principality?
– which seems to command everything, is in fact subordinate to
the second part: *how* are they acquired? The first space is thus
restricted and inflected by the second. Machiavelli's essential
question concerns the acquisition of principalities. Secondly, the
essential question concerns acquisition, not *beginnings*. As we
shall see, it includes the question of beginnings, but it seems
broader. Why? We shall have to explain this difference.

These two remarks having been made, following formulation
of the problem in Chapter I, the next ten chapters (II–XI) are
presented as an exhaustive inventory of *possible* kinds, *potential*
because real cases. One thinks of the Cartesian operation of
'complete enumeration', a speculative review. However, this

enumeration is once again performed by a method of *division* that calls to mind Plato's method in *The Sophist*, as we can see in Chapter I, where the plan of the first twelve chapters of *The Prince* seems to be announced. Principalities are divided into two kinds: (I) the 'hereditary' (acquired by right of inheritance) and (II) the *'new'*. The new in turn are divided into (1) the 'completely new' and (2) those *'like limbs joined to the hereditary state of the ruler who annexed them'*. The latter are acquired either (i) 'with the arms of others' or (ii) *'with one's own [arms]'*. And these latter are thus acquired either (a) 'through luck' or (b) *'through ability'*.[49] This is what Chapter I announces. Clearly, this division is not some plain and simple enumeration, but a classification which, through a series of divisions, 'paves the way', proceeding from the idea of the principality in general to the political idea (I mean politically exemplary and operative) of the *new* principality, and thence to the principality acquired 'with one's own arms', and through talent rather than luck.

But the reading of the chapters thus announced has a series of surprises in store for us.

The *first surprise* is the localization – one should say focalization – of the field of the problem. What is involved in the first twelve chapters of *The Prince* is definitely not an *abstract* general enumeration of possible cases, obtained by division, valid for all times and places. On the contrary, it is a list of *concrete* examples, concrete situations which constitute the *contemporary Italian conjuncture* and that of neighbouring countries (France and Spain). Some examples are indeed borrowed from antiquity, but their sole purpose is to supplement the contemporary Italian examples. The theory is presented, then, in a precise form: an analysis of the *Italian* conjunture, under the sway of the question: What are the conditions for the acquisition of a principality? And this question is implicitly or explicitly subordinate to another: What are the conditions of possibility for a New Principality that will endure and prove able to expand?

The *second surprise* is that the content of the chapters curiously exceeds what Chapter I announced. We find not only a short chapter in which Machiavelli demarcates himself from the *tyranny* of 'those who become rulers through wicked means' (Chapter VIII), but above all an astounding chapter on 'ecclesiastical principalities' (Chapter XI), of which it is said in two words that they have been acquired by *virtù* or luck, and which are thus – practically, if not theoretically – not on the inventory! They do not feature any the less in the analysis, and – the final straw – right at the end, in the last chapter, once all the cases have been inspected. Clearly, the ecclesiastical principalities figure on account of the Italian conjuncture, and it alone. But the way in which they are treated outside the inventory is evidence enough that they are *outside history*, and that Machiavelli expects nothing from them as regards attainment of his objective:

> [T]hey are sustained by ancient religious institutions . . . [their rulers] have states and do not defend them, and subjects whom they do not trouble to govern . . . since they are controlled by a higher power, which the human mind cannot comprehend, I shall refrain from discussing them. . . .[50]

Rather like republics. Rather like hereditary principalities, of which Machiavelli says only a few words in Chapter II. This is where some explanation is required.

Let us try to delimit our object. We have just eliminated a group of principalities: tyrannies, hereditary states, republics, and ecclesiastical principalities. Let us call this group I. What is left? Group II, on which Machiavelli is going to focus all his attention: namely, new principalities acquired by conquest, so-called *'mixed* principalities' (Chapter III); and *completely new* principalities, acquired either by someone else's arms or by one's own, by luck or *virtù*. What characterizes the principalities of group II is that they are *new*, regardless of whether the ruler is new (completely new principalities) or not (mixed principalities). Given this, how are the excluded principalities (group I) to be characterized? I would say – something Machiavelli himself does not specifically state, but which he thinks – that they are *old*, already *outdated*. To employ a formula that such modern commentators as Renaudet could have adopted from Gramsci,[51] let us say that Machiavelli can set up his political problem only on condition of *making a clean sweep of existing feudal forms as incompatible with the objective of Italian unity*. Tyranny is the reality of numerous minor Italian rulers, whether hereditary or otherwise. Machiavelli does not want tyranny, and ridicules hereditary legitimacy; the New Prince's titles do not derive from his bloodline. The ecclesiastical states – on which Machiavelli looses his fury in the *Discourses*, accusing them of having divided Italy and preventing its unity – are part and parcel of the feudal legacy, just like the nonchalant emperor who dispatches his armies to Italy from time to time. Nothing is to be expected of them. Machiavelli refuses to accept the precedence of religion over politics; he will place religion in the service of politics. Up to this point everything coheres. There remains the case of republics. Now, these are city-states formed into free communes, living off craft industry and trade, but irredeemably marked by feudal relations, organically incapable of extending their market over the national soil and resolving their political and economic problem with the surrounding countryside. They are *the urban forms of feudalism*, which Machiavelli, with surprising political insight, senses to be incapable of the economic transformation and expansion, and political conversion, that would make them suitable for the task of unifying the national state. He excludes them, just as he excludes all other *forms* of political existence and organization stamped by feudalism. He excludes them because they cannot furnish the political base from which Italian unity can and must be constructed. But he does not omit them from the political terrain on which this unity is to be achieved. This is why he devotes Chapter V to them: 'How one should govern cities or principalities that, before being conquered, used to live under their own laws'. Indeed, to constitute the national state it is imperative to conquer the nation bit by bit, and to conquer it over the whole range of its old principalities and tyrannies (hereditary or otherwise), ecclesiastical states, and free cities, starting out from a new political and military base. For they are inscribed in the configuration of the Italian conjuncture, and if nothing can be expected of them as regards constitution of the national state, it is imperative to conquer them. If it is impossible to construct the national state on the basis of feudal forms, that state must subordinate those forms to itself, conquer and transform them. They are its raw material.

Here, then, is how our object – the principalities of group II – is presented. Initially, it takes the form of the question of the conditions of possibility for conquest. The existence of a conquering principality is assumed in this question. But it is bracketed, and Machiavelli simply asks what happens when it annexes a principality, which is then not dubbed 'completely new' but, as 'a limb that is joined to another principality', 'almost mixed'.[52]

In fact, what is involved is principalities annexed by a more powerful state. This is a fundamental problem for the constitution of a nation, which can be born only by a first state extending its borders through conquest and annexation. The general question then posed is this: on what conditions is it possible to govern new territories – that is to say, what policy must the national Prince pursue when it comes to the annexation of new provinces? Here there is a capital distinction: 'I say, then, that the territories a conqueror annexes and joins to his own well-established state are either in the same *country*, with the same *language*, or they are not.'[53] If they are, things are straightforward. It is sufficient 'to wipe out the family of the ruler who held sway over them'. And as for the rest:

> [T]he inhabitants will continue to live quietly, provided their old way of life is maintained and there is no difference in customs. This has happened with Burgundy, Brittany, Gascony and Normandy, which have been joined to France for a long time. Although there are some linguistic differences, nevertheless their way of life is similar, so no difficulties have arisen.[54]

In other words, do 'not ... change their laws or impose new taxes. Then the old principality and the new territory will very soon become a single body politic.'[55] Examination of the alternative hypothesis – when the territories annexed are 'in a country that differs in language, customs and institutions'[56] – follows.

It is here that 'real difficulties' arise, because it is difficult to take root outside one's own country. Even so, one can try, says Machiavelli; but it is then necessary for the ruler either to go and live in the new territory, or to establish colonies there. This time all the examples are drawn from pure antiquity. The sole contemporary example, developed at length but wholly critical, is of French attempts to annex Italian territories: they have all misfired, and Machiavelli enumerates the five errors of 'King Louis' (XII), as if in the belief that they could have been avoided. It is impossible not to relate this analysis to the condemnation of foreign invasions of Italy. Why does Machiavelli moot this second hypothesis of a seemingly extra-national annexation? No doubt because the body of the nation is not fixed in advance, is in part aleatory – the stake of a struggle whose borders are not assigned – and because it is ultimately necessary to envisage annexation of territories with different languages and customs in order to embody the nation.

Machiavelli then comes to the heart of the matter, to the problem that has remained in suspense: the completely new principality that will have to conquer the others to constitute the nation. This is dealt with in Chapters VI ('New principalities acquired by one's own arms and ability') and VII ('New principalities acquired through the power of others and their favour'). Here it is expressly a question of 'completely new principalit[ies], where there is a new ruler', and of 'completely new principalities, both as regards the ruler and the type of government'.[57] And so it is here that the political and theoretical pair of the New Principality and the New Prince, which we glimpsed on the horizon of Machiavelli's whole problematic, emerges into the open, and with it the theme of beginnings.

A new principality poses such 'difficulties' that in order to found one it is necessary to emulate 'skilful archers ... when their target seems too distant': 'knowing well the power of their bow, they aim at a much higher point, not to hit it with the arrow, but by aiming there to be able to strike their target'.[58] *To aim at a much higher point*: for Machiavelli, this is explicitly to emulate the greatest examples in history – Moses, Cyrus, Romulus, Theseus, and so on. But to aim at a much higher point has a further sense, not spelt out, but practised, by Machiavelli: to aim at a much higher point = to aim *beyond what exists*, so as to attain a goal *that does not exist* but must exist = to aim above all existing principalities, beyond their *limits*.

What does the difficulty consist in? In the fact that everything is new, that the processes of becoming-the-Prince and becoming-the-Principality are one and the same: the process of the new development, the beginning. The Prince does not pre-exist the New Principality; the New Principality does not precede the New Prince. They must begin together, and this beginning is what Machiavelli calls an 'adventure': 'this adventure of passing from private citizen to ruler'.[59] Echoing this formula, we might say: 'this adventure of passing from "geographical expression" to national state'.

Let us try to classify the *conditions* for this adventure, without losing sight of the fact that it involves the foundation of a New Principality with an eminent vocation. There are three.

The *first general condition*, defining this adventure, is to assume the form of a favourable *'encounter'* between two terms: on the one hand, the objective conditions of the conjuncture X of an unspecified region – *fortuna* – and on the other, the subjective conditions of an equally indeterminate individual Y – *virtù*.

This encounter can transpire in three forms:

(a) *Correspondence: the limit-form*, that is to say, the most favourable. This comprises correspondence between good fortune in the conjuncture – that is to say, an auspicious 'opportunity', 'matter' ready to receive a form[60] – and *virtù* in the individual – political *virtù*, which consists in determining what shape to give the pre-existing material in order to found a durable principality.

This limit-form involves *correspondence* between *fortuna* and *virtù*. The other forms are (b) non-correspondence; and (c) deferred and restored correspondence.

(b) *Non-correspondence: negative form*. In this case we are dealing with a different kind of situation, in which *fortuna* does everything – as regards conjuncture and individual alike – but *the individual is not endowed with corresponding virtù*. Here the individual cannot survive the fortune which, for example, has temporarily brought him to power, since fortune changes: he will not be able to found a state – or, at any rate, a state that endures.

(c) *Deferred correspondence*. By contrast, an individual can benefit from an extravagant fortune at the outset. *Fortuna* once again takes charge of everything, without the *virtù* of the individual having any hand in it. But if the individual favoured by *fortuna* has political *virtù*, he will then be able *to recapture this sheer fortuna by his virtù*, transform the fortune of an instant into political duration via *virtù* and, for example, subsequently furnish his state with the 'foundations' he failed to supply at the outset.

As we can see, everything revolves around the *encounter and non-encounter*, the correspondence and non-correspondence, of *fortuna* and *virtù*. If this correspondence, whether immediate or deferred, is not ensured – in other words, in the absence of this encounter – there is no New Prince and no New Principality.

The *second condition* extends this general law to the particular case of the individual who, in order to make a beginning, resorts to the *power of others* – let us say, to the case of a man who, to found a New Principality, starts out by relying on the armies of a foreign ruler, as did Cesare Borgia when he summoned the King of France to his aid and secured his first victories with French troops. With due alteration of detail, this recourse to the power of another plays the same role vis-à-vis *virtù* as *fortuna*. And once again, two cases present themselves.

First case: if the individual who calls on the power of others for aid possesses no political *virtù* – if he is unable to *recapture*, by intrinsic *virtù*, the extrinsic conditions of his initial success – he will be incapable of rapidly emancipating himself from the foreign forces he needed and furnishing 'his own forces'. He is lost, for he cannot but succumb to servitude to others. He cannot found a state that endures.

Second case: if, on the other hand, the individual who starts out depending on someone else's forces possesses the requisite *virtù* to liberate himself and fashion his own forces, then he can become his master, *master his beginnings*, and found a state that endures. If he can master this initial dependence, as in the case of *fortuna*, this will be by *virtù*: 'For . . . a man who does not lay his foundations at first may be able to do it later, if he possesses great ability, although this creates difficulties for the builder and the edifice itself may well prove unstable.'[61]

The *third condition* is the effect of the encounter/correspondence: the conversion of *fortuna* into *virtù*, the casting of *fortuna* as *virtù*. . . . In the case of the foundation of a New Principality by a New Prince, the encounter between *fortuna* and *virtù* has a very specific political meaning in Machiavelli, indicated in Chapter VII and illustrated by the classical examples of Chapter VI. The peculiarity of *virtù* is to master *fortuna*, even when it is favourable, and to transform the instant of *fortuna* into political duration, the *matter* of *fortuna* into political *form*, and thus to structure the material of the favourable local conjuncture politically by laying the foundations of the new state – that is to say, by rooting itself (we know how) in the people, in order to endure and expand, while remaining ever mindful of 'future power' and aiming high to reach far.

I leave to one side the purely philosophical implications of this astonishing theory of the interplay of *fortuna* and *virtù* (= encounter, matter/form, correspondence/non-correspondence). Through these general variations, a specific theory of the conditions for the great 'adventure' of the foundation of a New Principality by a New Prince is sketched. *Fortuna* must arrange the 'matter' that is to receive a form. At the same time, an individual must emerge who is endowed with *virtù* – capable, should he have to resort to them, of emancipating himself from dependency on another's forces so as to fashion his own by *virtù*; and finally capable of laying 'very strong foundations for his future power',[62] by rooting himself in the people through *virtù*.

Here we have the crucial point of this theory, where politics appears in person: *in the form of a determinate absence.* Formally, the theory is presented as an absolutely *general* theory, a theory of the *fortuna/virtù* encounter, and the variations of correspondence/non-correspondence between its terms: an *abstract* theory. This abstract generality can be seen in the fact that if Machiavelli defines the two terms *fortuna* and *virtù*, and the law of their corresponding and non-corresponding encounter, he leaves the names of the protagonists in this encounter *completely blank*; he provides them with no *identity*. The geographical space where the encounter is to occur, and the individual who is to encounter *fortuna* there, have no name: by definition, they are *unknown*. Not unknown like the unknown quantities of an equation, x, y, where it suffices to solve the equation to know [*sic*]. They are absolute unknowns because Machiavelli says nothing about them. In which bit of Italy will the encounter occur? Machiavelli does not say. Which individual endowed with *virtù* will know how to seize hold of the *fortuna* that presents itself, and impart form to the matter aspiring to it? Machiavelli does not say. He seems to take refuge in a general theory, and wait for history to perform.

In my opinion, however, it would be a mistake to identify the anonymity of the protagonists of this theory with its generality and abstraction. Indeed, I believe the following thesis can be defended: this anonymity is in no way an effect of theoretical abstraction but, on the contrary, a political condition and objective, inscribed in the theory. In other words, the *abstract* form of the theory is the index and effect of a *concrete* political stance. To understand it, it is enough to recall what was said of the principalities that make up group II, which covers practically *all* Italian principalities. This stance can then be summarized thus: Italian national unity cannot be ensured starting out from any of the Italian states – either in or under any of the political forms of *any* existing Italian state – or by *any* of the existing princes in the existent principalities. If Machiavelli evokes the theme of novelty and beginnings with such insistence, if he speaks of a New Prince in a New Principality, it is because he rejects all existing states and rulers as *old* – that is to say, feudal, orientated towards the past, outmoded, incapable of this task for the future. He rejects them all on account of their historical impotence. But at the same time he puts in place the protocols and forms for the encounter between a propitious conjuncture and a *virtuoso* individual: an encounter that is possible and necessary. He does not, however, supply any name, or place, or man. This silence possesses a positive political sense. It means that this encounter will occur, but outside *existing* states and rulers; hence *somewhere* in Italy, in a bit of Italy that cannot be an existing state – an encounter between *fortuna* and an anonymous individual, who is not required to be a prince already, only to be capable of becoming such.

It might be thought that this conception is utterly utopian, and that the condition attached to the history of Italian unity by Machiavelli – that it will begin with the rejection of all existing political forms and hence that it will start from nothing – is a reverie. In reality, for Machiavelli these conditions are political imperatives over which no compromise is possible, since he who does not respect them will succumb to the past, the sway of the existing states and their impotence. But Machiavelli further considers that these conditions, far from being a reverie, are perfectly attainable. The proof? They have had the sanction of historical reality. Staggering as it may be, *the beginning has already occurred*. In an Italian province that was not a state, an individual who was not a ruler created a New Principality and was a New Prince: Cesare Borgia.

'I do not know what better precepts to offer a new ruler than to cite his actions as a pattern', writes Machiavelli.[63] In fact, the Duke's adventure realizes, in all its purity, the hypothesis of the absolute beginning – at once completely necessary and completely unforeseeable – of a New Prince and a New Principality, capable of enhancing their power to the point of aspiring to Italian unity. The son of Pope Alexander VI, Cesare is certainly not a commoner. But this boy, cardinal and archbishop at the age of sixteen, is not a prince in a state. It so happens that he renounces his ecclesiastical titles to seek his fortune in the secular world. Politically, he is nothing. For want of anything else, his father offers him a piece of the Papal States, a scrap of territory at the outermost bounds, in the Romagna: a place that is not a state, in a political domain bereft of any structure, since it is one of those states wherein there is neither prince who rules, nor subjects who are ruled – and, moreover, part of the Papal States. Cesare is going to make a new state out of this politically *shapeless* site and material, and become its New Prince. His political practice combines all the requisite features for success. He starts out with good luck, but in order to transform it into a durable structure through his *virtù*. He begins by getting the help of the King of France, but in order to dispense with his services as rapidly as possible and constitute his own forces; this he achieves by arming his subjects, the men of the territories he conquers and wins over. He wins them over by providing them with a good administration, 'efficient government'. If he employs the worst methods of fraud and villainy, it is solely for the purpose of achieving his independence, winning the people's favour, and defeating the enemies opposed to his expansion. Soon he has made himself master of the whole of Romagna and the Marches, is intent on the conquest of Bologna, and crosses the Apennines to invade Pisa and Florence. A kingdom is taking shape that is on the point of occupying central Italy and extending from the Adriatic to the Mediterranean, under an irresistible Prince who seems to possess the stature and *virtù* of a future king of Italy. At all events, Cesare has handled matters in conformity with Machiavelli's principles, combining luck and use of another's forces with his own political and military *virtù*. Until the day *fortuna* turned against him: 'And he told me himself, on the day Julius II was elected, that he had thought about what might happen when his father died, and had provided against everything, except that he had never thought that, when his father was dying, he too would be at death's door.'[64] This mortal agony, this fever caught in the swamps that laid him at death's door for two months, when his father had just died, was fatal to him. He needed to intervene at this moment, but could not: his whole edifice collapsed, and Cesare disappeared to go and die in obscurity in the service of the King of Navarre, under the walls of a small Spanish square.[65] An event that opens another chapter: that of the absolute *limits* beyond which it is no longer possible to master *fortuna*.

When Machiavelli wrote *The Prince*, in 1513, Cesare had departed the Italian scene some seven years previously, and strictly speaking nothing remained of his work. Nothing but his example. Yet the fact of this example is capital; for he is the material, empirical proof of the conditions of possibility for the realization of the New Prince in a New Principality in the forms conceived by Machiavelli. He is empirical proof that the formulation of Machiavelli's problem is correct – and, in particular, that it is politically necessary and correct to leave undefined – in anonymity, and hence abstraction – both the *birthplace* of the New Principality and the *surname* of the New Prince, while defining with *extreme precision* the forms of the encounter between the conjuncture and the exceptional individual, as well as the political practice[66] through which this individual is going to constitute himself as Prince, and constitute as principality the place wherein he establishes himself and whence he is going to expand.

Far from contradicting this anonymity, the example of Cesare, who sets out from the Romagna, is proof of its correctness. For who could have foreseen that it would be Cesare, and that he would set out from the Romagna? What the example of Cesare proves is that *the New Prince can start from anywhere, and be anyone: ultimately start from nothing, and be nothing to start with.* Once again, nothingness – or, rather, the aleatory void.[67]

The empirical, historical example of Cesare thus proves with crystal clarity that a completely New Prince in a completely New Principality is materially *possible*, and hence that it is not a dream or utopia. And since, for Machiavelli, this new beginning is the absolute condition of Italian unity; and since it is necessary, to set the process of Italian unity in train, to *make a clean sweep of the past* – that is to say, of every existing principality – Cesare's existence is proof that the political conditions for Italian unity are not only necessary, but also possible. The anonymous character of the theory then assumes its full political significance: the abstraction of the theory of the *encounter* is not merely a theoretical abstraction here. The place and interplay of this *abstraction* impart a *concrete* political function to it; in fact, the abstraction of anonymity is simultaneously the clean sweep of the past and its consequence: namely, that the great adventure begins apart from everything that actually exists, hence in an unkown place with an unknown man.[68]

But we are then in the presence of an exceptional form of thought. On the one hand, we have conditions specified with the utmost precision, from the general state of the Italian conjuncture to the forms of the encounter between *fortuna* and *virtù*, and the exigencies of the process of political practice. On the other, we have a total lack of specification as to the site and subject of political practice. The striking thing is that Machiavelli firmly grasps both ends of the chain – in short, thinks and formulates this theoretical disjuncture, this 'contradiction', without wishing to propose any kind of theoretical reduction or resolution of it, whether notional or oneiric. This thinking of the disjuncture stems from the fact that Machiavelli not only formulates, but thinks, his problem *politically* – that is to say, as a contradiction in reality that cannot be removed by thought, but only by reality. It can be removed only by the sudden appearance – necessary, but unforeseeable and inascribable as regards place, time and person – of the *concrete* forms of the political *encounter* whose general conditions alone are defined. In this theory that ponders and preserves the disjuncture, room is thereby made for political practice. Room is made for it through this organization of disjoined theoretical notions, by the discrepancy between the definite and indefinite, the necessary and the unforeseeable. This discrepancy, thought and unresolved by thought, is the presence of history and political practice in theory itself.

Here I halt an exposition that has led us, via the *Discourses* and *The Prince*, to recognize the theoretical problem on which Machiavelli's whole reflection is focused: namely, the beginnings of a state that endures, the conditions for the foundation and duration of this state – a problem that takes the political form of the New Prince. As we have just seen, this problem is posed in theoretical forms that prioritize political practice in person.

The Political Practice of the New Prince

The New Prince's political practice is, of course, expounded after the first eleven chapters of *The Prince* we have just analysed. It is dealt with in Chapters XII–XXIII.

In this analysis, Machiavelli puts aside the problem of the original founding moment for practical purposes, since it cannot be localized. He assumes that things have already begun, and that the conjoint process of becoming-the-Prince and becoming-the-state is under way. The issue he poses and treats is the political *practice* that the Prince must employ to see this process through to a successful conclusion in the first instance.

To understand Machiavelli's theory, three points need to be made.

1. The state is led by a Prince, but the Prince's practice is unintelligible if it is not appreciated that this state is a state rooted in the people, *a popular state*. The popular character of the state determines the Prince's political practice.
2. What is involved in the Prince's political practice is not the state in the broad sense – namely, the social organization of a people in all its manifestations: economic, political, and so on. It is the state in the narrow, political sense as a form of state power, as *state power* held by an individual and exercised by what the Marxist tradition has called the *state apparatus*. When Machiavelli analyses the Prince's political practice, he analyses the practice of the holder of *state power*, and therefore analyses the *means* that he fashions or employs, constitutes

and implements, in order to exercise state power – in other words, what we can call the state apparatus.

3. This state, of which Machiavelli says somewhere that it is a 'machine', can, at first sight, be divided into three elements: at one extreme, the apparatus of force, represented by the *army*; at the other, the apparatus of *consent*, represented by religion and the entire system of ideas that the people forms of the Prince; and, between the two, the *politico–juridical* apparatus represented by the 'system of laws', the provisional outcome and institutional framework of the struggle between social classes. I am only just stretching the Machiavellian definitions, so as to inscribe them in a terminology that obviously anticipates Marxist theory. In Machiavelli the instruments of force (i.e. the army), the instruments of consent (i.e. religion and the Prince's reputation), and the instruments for the 'channelling' of conflicting humours (i.e. laws), are *component parts* of the state; they constitute its means, substance and mechanism. To be a New Prince is at one and the same time to know how to fashion these instruments of state power (the army) or seize hold of them (religion), and to utilize them to realize a popular politics. It is because these three instruments feature in the state, and in particular because force does not figure there alone but combines with laws and popular consent, that the state is the converse of a tyranny, and hence can be popular. This was clearly appreciated by Gramsci, who discovered in the combination of force and consent notions that referred him back to the Marxist definition of the state: 'hegemony [consent] protected by the armour of coercion [force]'.[1]

Laws have already been discussed. We shall therefore leave them aside and concentrate on the other two elements: the army and ideology.

Machiavelli's theses on the army are impressive – not only in their consistency, but above all for their incisiveness and political acuteness. They anticipate not only the Jacobin positions of the French Revolution, but also the well-known theses of Clausewitz, Engels and Mao Zedong on armies and war. Obviously, Machiavelli speaks a language whose terminology is not identical to that of the Jacobins or the Marxists. But his principal theses

are incisive, and of an astonishing political and theoretical penetration. To clarify what follows, I shall group them together in
four essential theses.

First thesis: the army is the number-one, *quintessential state
apparatus*, constituting the state as force, endowing it with a *real*
material – i.e. historical and political – existence.[2] A Prince
without an army is merely an unarmed prophet, like Savano-
rola.[3] However much he resorted to religion; to *ideology*, let us
say – that is, the other essential attribute of state power – he
lacked the absolute precondition, the number-one attribute, of
state power: the state apparatus of *armed force*.[4] 'Consequently,
all armed prophets succeed whereas unarmed ones fail.'[5] The
contrast between armed and unarmed prophets illustrates and
fixes the contrast between a ruler who relies *exclusively* on
ideology or laws – who, by one means or another, enjoys popular
support, but does not possess armed force – and another ruler
who does possess armed force and can, in addition, rely on laws
and popular ideology. The former is doomed to defeat; the latter
can be hopeful of victory. This brings out the double function of
the state – of force and ideological consent – but under the
primacy of force: hence *the primacy of the army as state apparatus
over ideology and laws*.

Second thesis: the army, its constitution, formation and utilization, must be considered predominantly from the viewpoint of
politics. To revert to two famous formulas, it is necessary (1) to
regard war as the continuation of politics by other means; and
(2) to 'put politics in command' in military matters.[6] Machiavelli
is the first conscious, explicit and consistent theorist of the *primacy
of the political over the military* in military matters themselves; of
the primacy of politics over military technique. Machiavelli is
the first theorist consciously and systematically to subordinate
technical questions regarding armies and war to the primacy of
politics. To give some idea of this, Machiavelli is, for example,
famous for having rejected as erroneous the celebrated maxim
that wealth is the sinews of warfare: for him, the sinews of
warfare are good soldiers.[7] Machiavelli is equally well known
for having subjected the use of castles and fortresses to a radical
critique: they are not solutions because they are political mistakes. Fortresses are a monument not to architecture, but to political error. Castles of brick and iron are dangerous expedients:

a ruler's real citadels are his people, his soldiers, his people in arms.[8] To take another example: Machiavelli is known for having denounced the ideology of contemporary military experts, who believed that the ultimate weapon of artillery was going to overturn all the rules of war. Against them Machiavelli maintained that *virtù* – political and military valour – would always have the last word on the battlefield, even if – especially if – the intervention of artillery had the effect of *compelling* soldiers to engage in *close combat*.[9]

Third thesis: We have stated two successive theses. The first asserted the primacy of force over consent, the *primacy of the army* over ideology, in the state. Now, we have just seen that in respect of this same army, the second thesis asserted the *primacy of politics*. The first thesis is thus subordinate to the second, which imparts its true meaning to it. To have stuck to the first thesis would, in effect, have been to reduce state power to the exercise of naked force, to the technical employment of the army, combined with the subsidiary effects of consent. The second thesis rectifies this potential error, since it defines force, the army, as subordinate to politics. The upshot is that armed force is simply the realization of politics in the region of the state that employs violence. Now, *the same politics* is realized in laws and ideology. The force/consent, army/ideology, duality is thus not an antagonistic one: it is not a case of violence on the one hand, persuasion on the other. This duality realizes two necessary forms of state power under a single rule: that of the Prince's popular and national politics.

Fourth thesis: the system thus specified – the unity of armed force, laws and forms of popular consent, hence the system of military and ideological politics in the popular state – can be characterized by a slogan that commands everything: the Prince must *rely on his own forces*. Let us take this to mean his forces in the narrow sense – his army – and his forces in the broad sense. They are one and the same: the Prince's forces are those of his people. The Prince must fashion forces that are his, his own, strictly his own; he must rely on his own forces, count on his own forces, be 'the complete master of his own forces'.[10] Such is Machiavelli's constant refrain. We have seen the general sense of this thesis in the relationship between *fortuna* and *virtù*. We are now going to observe it directly at work in military policy.

Once these indicators have been offered, the Machiavellian theory of the New Prince's army – one should say: the theory of the New Army – can be understood without difficulty. But it contains some surprises. Here are the essential moments.

Since in all things a clean sweep must be made of the past – not the classical examples of antiquity, but current forms pertaining to the outmoded past – Machiavelli begins by rejecting three types of troops or army that share a single and unique feature: namely, that in their case the Prince cannot count on his own forces, his 'own troops'.[11] These three types of army are mercenaries, auxiliaries, and mixed troops. The second part of *The Prince* begins at Chapter XII with their rejection.

Mercenaries are 'useless' and 'dangerous'.[12] Why? Because they are retained solely by *money*:

> [T]hey have no affection for you or any other reason to induce them to fight for you, except a trifling wage, which is not sufficient to make them want to risk their lives for you. They are very glad to be in your service as long as you do not wage war, but in time of war they either flee or desert.[13]

Accordingly, they are useless. But they are also dangerous. For if they chance to have a good mercenary leader, he can turn them against the Prince. And if they do not turn against the Prince, they form bands that proceed to pillage the country.

Auxiliary troops are 'much more dangerous than mercenaries',[14] since they are not even dependent upon the Prince for their wage. They are dispatched by a foreign ruler; they have *another master*, triggering another sequence of events:[15] 'In themselves, these auxiliaries can be capable and effective but they are almost always harmful to those who use them; for if they lose you will be ruined, and if you win you will be at their mercy.'[16] So true is this that it is preferable 'to lose using [your] own troops ... than to conquer through using foreign troops', for 'weapons and armour belonging to others fall off you or weigh you down or constrict your movements'.[17]

In the case of mercenaries, they have no master at all; they are not of the people, but are retained solely by money, which only encourages them to pillage and cannot bind them either to their employer or to his country.

In the case of auxiliaries, they have a master and a country, but it is not the Prince: it is someone else. They are bound to their external master, and he who resorts to them is caught in another's trap: if he relies on someone else's troops, he is liable to be delivered over to his political designs. This is why auxiliaries are even more dangerous than mercenaries.

Mixed armies comprise native and mercenary troops. An example is France. Charles VII was able to liberate France from the English because 'he recognised the need for France to be defended by national troops, and formed an army composed of cavalry and infantry'.[18] But his son Louis XI abolished the infantry and hired Swiss as infantrymen. This was a serious blunder, for in 'disband[ing] the infantry [he] made his own cavalry dependent on foreign soldiers' (we shall see where the infantry comes in later):

> The French armies, then, have been of a mixed character, partly mercenary and partly national. Such a combination is much better than an army of auxiliaries or an army of mercenaries *but much inferior to native troops.* And let this example suffice: for the Kingdom of France would be unconquerable if the military system set up by Charles had been developed or, at least, preserved.[19]

In decreasing order of disadvantage, then, there are four types of army: *auxiliaries* and *mercenaries* – both definitively condemned, this condemnation being accompanied by numerous examples from the history of Italy, whose rulers committed the unpardonable blunder of trusting in them; then the intermediate form of *mixed armies*, which are *part native, part mercenary*; and finally, *purely national armies* – the only good ones. Understanding that it will have to come down to them, and them alone, is the absolute precondition of being a New Prince. Here again Cesare Borgia can serve as proof:

> This Duke invaded the Romagna using auxiliaries (all his troops being *French*). . . . But since he distrusted them, he used mercenaries. . . . When he later found them to be of doubtful value and loyalty, and therefore dangerous, he disbanded them and formed an army composed of *his own men*.[20]

He then became 'the complete master of his own forces', and thus implemented Machiavelli's critique, producing his conclusion in practice.[21]

What is an army of one's own? '[O]ne's own forces are those

composed of subjects or citizens or of one's dependents; all the others are either mercenaries or auxiliaries.'[22] The New Army will therefore be a *popular* army. This involves not merely a generic denomination, but a political determination. Machiavelli's notion consists not simply in rejecting mercenaries or someone else's weapons, but in a new political conception of the army's *recruitment* and *organization*.

To constitute a popular army is to arm a section of the population that had not hitherto possessed weapons. Furthermore, it is to have the people in arms play a new role in the army's organization and operation. This objective is attained by two measures:

1. Recruitment of the army from the popular strata of town and country, in the form of standing popular militias. Machiavelli's essential innovation in this respect is massively to extend recruitment to the *peasantry*, and to have them enrol in the standing militias. This constitutes the blending of town and country.
2. A reorganization of the army that ensures a preponderance of infantry over cavalry. This represents the primacy of infantry.

On these two counts Machiavelli overturns prevailing opinion, and introduces revolutionary innovations whose political import is obvious. It involves imparting a popular content to the army and, at the same time, making it the school and crucible of popular unity, by reversing the political balance of forces within it. To have peasants enrol in the army *en masse* undermines the power of the feudal lords. To unite the popular strata of town and country in the infantry, and prioritize it over cavalry, initiates a process of social and political amalgamation that simultaneously challenges the hierarchies sanctioned by the feudal order and its military organization. Not only does the lofty reign of the cavalryman come to an end, but a new form of popular unity, hitherto nonexistent, takes shape: in the army common to them, the men of the towns and countryside begin to become – learn to become – one and the same people. Gramsci was especially sensitive to this political objective of Machiavelli's:

Any formation of national-popular collective will is impossible, unless the great mass of peasant farmers bursts simultaneously into political life. That was Machiavelli's intention through the reform of the militia, and it was achieved by the Jacobins in the French Revolution. That Machiavelli understood it reveals a precocious Jacobinism that is the (more or less fertile) germ of his conception of national revolution.[23]

The conception of the army in Machiavelli then appears in all its clarity and truly revolutionary audacity. I should like to underscore the impressive political logic of Machiavelli's approach. To indicate it clearly, its moments must be itemized.

In a *first moment*, we learnt and appreciated that the army was to serve to build the new state – that is to say, serve as a means to national and popular ends. But it was open to us to think that the relation of means to ends was one of *exteriority*, the army being a neutral technical instrument, a force organized according to the rules of existing military technique and serving authority purely as a means to attainment of its ends. Machiavelli plunges us into a quite different universe. The existing army, the forms of its employment, recruitment and organization, all existing military techiques – these he condemns and repudiates as *politically incompatible* with attainment of his political objective. To this new end, a new army is required, one that is politically compatible with that new goal and, like it, popular and national.

This is the *second moment*, when Machiavelli declares that the Prince equips himself with forces that are his own and, to fashion them, must arm his own subjects. On this condition, the means – the army – will no longer be external to the end – the nation – since the army will be national. This already represents a significant result. Yet Machiavelli's strongest point does not lie here. Indeed, one might make do with the slogan: national army, national because recruited from the Prince's subjects! One might rest content with this *generality*, without searching for what I would call the specific material[24] *forms* of organization that are going to transform this formally national army into an authentically national army. If one goes no further than this generality, a relation of exteriority between army and political goal necessarily persists; the army is no longer alien to the goal, but it remains a means to an end external to it.

But here is the *third moment*, when we discover that the *forms* of army recruitment and organization have the effect of making the end internal to the army itself; and that creation of the army is already in itself accomplishment of the goal. *Not only are the means not external to the end, but the end is internal to the means.* For Machiavelli's army – with its popular recruitment, amalgamation of town and country, and supremacy of infantry over cavalry – forms and already unites the people whom the state is assigned the goal of uniting and expanding, simply by virtue of being constituted. The army can serve as a means to a political end only if it is already the realized form of the relevant politics. The sheer existence of Machiavelli's army is something quite different from a means to solve a problem: it is already in itself the resolution of this problem. Therewith Machiavelli advances the remarkable claim that the requisite means for the resolution of a problem must already be *in themselves* – realize in themselves – the resolution of that problem. On the political level this position takes the following paradoxical form: the army – which is force in the state and, as such, can be contrasted with forms of consent or distinguished from them – is not only a force. It is also, and conjointly, an institution that acts socially and politically on the attitudes of the soldiers and people – an institution that shapes consent. The military apparatus simultaneously exercises an ideological function. Ideology thus figures in the army itself, as the Prince's other means of power.

Machiavelli's conviction is that there is no escaping the reign of men's opinion, beliefs and judgements. Political relations have two aspects: on one side is force, on the other, opinion. In Machiavelli it is not a matter of such and such an individual's opinion. His purpose is not to elaborate an anthropology or psychology of individual passions and opinions. His target is the mass: *'il volgo'*. He states it categorically: 'the common people are the vast majority' (we shall take 'common people' to be the popular masses). The only object that could be of concern to the Prince's political practice is the opinion of the people in its mass: *'il volgo'* ('[f]or the common people are impressed by appearances and results. Everywhere the common people are the vast majority, and the few are isolated when the majority and the government are at one'[25]).

In Machiavelli the problem of political ideology and the political practice of ideology is centred on two themes, one of which – religion – is relatively straightforward, whereas the other – the representation of the Prince's person in popular opinion – is highly complex.

Machiavelli starts out from religion as a given which it is absolutely impossible to ignore, since it is the existing dominant mass ideology. But he does not accept it at face value. He categorically does not confront religion with the question of its origin and religious credentials. He considers it from an exclusively political, factual point of view,[26] as an instrument, alongside the army, for the foundation, constitution and duration of the state. He treats it as an existing reality defined by its political function. As before, he simply poses it the political question of the conditions and forms of its utilization and transformation.

Machiavelli discusses religion in Book I of the *Discourses*, immediately after elaborating his theory of the foundation of a new state by a single individual, and devotes several chapters to the Romans' religion. His basic theme is as follows. Romulus had only laid the initial foundations of Rome and designed its laws; it still remained to secure the people's obedience and 'mould' it: 'Having found a very fierce people and wishing to bring them to civil obedience with the arts and peace, [Numa Pompilius] turned to religion as [an] *absolutely necessary* [support] for maintaining a civilized society.'[27] The text goes on to show the function of religion: it is the precondition for military and legal obedience and, through recourse to 'God's authority', induces the people to accept the introduction of new institutions, as well as the crucial decisions required at critical moments. Thus, it is because they knew how to makes themselves masters of the art of manipulating oracles – and, on the eve of battles, interpreting the behaviour of sacred fowl not always desirous of pecking! – that Roman kings, consuls and commanders could secure the support of the people or soldiers. I cannot go into the detail of these often extremely mordant examples, where Machiavelli is even more cyncial than his historical models.

If we want to understand the meaning of these arguments, we must analyse the formula stating that religion is an 'absolutely necessary [support] for maintaining a civilized society'. Why 'support'? Why 'absolutely necessary'? The term 'support' designates religion's ideological function. Religion rallies the people to existing institutions; it secures their obedience and submission to military and legal regulations. This adhesion, this popular consent, is indispensable to the functioning of the army and laws. 'Without religion, no army or laws' signifies: without the support of ideology, no popular consent to the state. It is indeed a question of ideology, since religion elicits such popular consent without violence, in and through the simple idea and *fear* of the gods:

> Just as the observance of divine worship is the cause of the greatness of republics, so the disregard of divine worship is the cause of their ruin, because where fear of God is lacking, that kingdom must either come to ruin or be sustained through fear of a prince who makes up for the shortcomings in its religion.[28]

So the essence of religion is fear, which, as we shall see, is the most economical (!) and reliable form of ideology. But at the same time religion is the most *necessary* support because, when it comes to fear, fear of the gods has the immense advantage over fear of the Prince that it is *constant*, not exposed to the vicissitudes of the political existence of an individual who might not only die, but also commit blunders.

Hence the fundamental political rule:

> The rulers of a republic or a kingdom must . . . uphold the foundations of the religion they profess; and having done this, they will find it an easy matter for them to maintain a devout republic and, as a consequence, one that is good and united. They must also encourage and support all those things that arise in favour of this religion, even those they judge to be false. . . .[29]

Considering the volley of blows Machiavelli delivered to the Papal States, and what he regarded as the papacy's political *treason*, it will be appreciated that these lines on religion are truly those of a great politician.

I leave to one side a whole series of important problems. These are connected with the primacy of politics and the state over religion, especially the denunciation of the Roman Catholic Church's treason against the Christian religion ('[w]e Italians have . . . this initial debt to the church and to the priests, that we have become irreligious'[30]); and with the definition of the genuine religion dreamed of by Machiavelli for his state – a religion inspired by Rome, a properly political religion, a religion that forms men not for abnegation and weakness but for strength and action – in short, *virtù*.

From them a certain conception of religion emerges, as two-dimensional, mass political and moral ideology: on the one hand, *fear*, keeping subjects obedient; on the other, *virtù*, inspiring them to conduct and action worthy of the state.

Religion thereby performs, as it were, the role of a *basic ideology*, a general, constant ideology against whose background the very particular ideology involving the relations between people and Prince stands out, in the form of the representation of the Prince in popular opinion.

In effect, it can be said that in Machiavelli the representation of the Prince in popular opinion is a veritable *means* of state power, and that on this account it may be regarded as part of state ideology, not to say *ideological state apparatus*.[31]

To understand the mechanism of this representation, we must go behind the stage, the performance, and discover the actor: the Prince. What is the Prince?

The Prince is not some ordinary, private individual. We recall Machiavelli's little phrase on the 'adventure' involved in making the transition from private individual to Prince. This process of becoming-a-Prince demands prolonged practice. But in his essence, even as a novice, the Prince is no longer a private individual: he is a political individual, wholly defined by his political function, by the necessary existence of the state in the guise of an individual, the individual existence of the state.

The private individual seeks satisfaction of his needs or passions; he is subject to the categories of religion and morality. He is judged according to the terms of the moral alternative: vices/virtues. His perfection is defined by moral virtue.

For his part, the Prince belongs to a different realm of existence. It is not satisfaction of his needs that motivates him, or assuagement of his passions that should guide him. He is beyond the moral categories of vice and virtue. For he pursues a completely distinct goal: a historical goal – founding, consolidating and expanding a state that endures. His perfection resides not in *moral virtue*, but in *political virtù* – that is to say, in the excellence of all the political virtues – of character, intelligence, etc. – appropriate to accomplishment of his task.

At this level of existence, the Prince can be judged by only one criterion: *success*. The adage 'the result alone counts' can be literally applied to him in all its rigour. This is so, however, on condition that it is understood that the result is itself defined by the Prince's historical task – that it is only *this* result that counts, not some other. Only the result that conforms to this task counts; all the rest are condemned. We are at the antipodes of any vulgar pragmatism. The result alone counts: but the *goal* is the sole arbiter of the result that counts.

It is from this perspective that the relation between political *virtù* and moral virtue and vice can be considered. *Virtù* is not the opposite of moral virtue: it is *of a different order*. It does not exclude moral virtue; *virtù* is so positioned vis-à-vis virtue that it can include it, yet simultaneously *exceed* it. Thus, *virtù* can take the form of moral virtue. But it must then be said that *the Prince is morally virtuous through political virtù*, and Machiavelli would like him to be so as often as possible.

But *virtù* is so positioned relative to virtue that it makes the Prince 'prepared to act immorally',[32] as Machiavelli puts it – even capable of committing a crime, a parricide [*sic*] (Romulus), an assassination, a breach of trust (Borgia), and so on. Once again, it is the result alone that counts – that is to say, the historical task with which we are acquainted. Thus, 'it cannot be called virtue [*virtù*] to kill one's fellow-citizens, to betray one's friends, to be treacherous, merciless and irreligious', writes Machiavelli of Agathocles' 'appallingly cruel and inhumane conduct, and countless wicked deeds'.[33] Machiavelli returns to this theme in connection with cruelty. When it is employed continuously, it goes on increasing, in a spiral of violence, and is bad. By contrast, when, at the state's inception, it is imperative to strike a blow, cruelty may be necessary and good:

> [Cruel deeds] may be called well committed (if one may use the word 'well' of that which is evil) when they are all committed at once, because they are necessary for establishing one's power, and are not afterwards persisted in, but changed for measures as beneficial as possible to one's subjects.[34]

Founding the state, seeking and achieving the well-being of one's subjects: this is the result that counts and judges *virtù*, as it judges the moral virtues and vices the Prince has assumed and practised by *virtù*. Moral as often as possible, immoral when the political result dictates it, but always out of *virtù*: moral by *virtù*, immoral by *virtù* – such is the Prince, that singular individual who is not a private citizen. This is why the *virtù* of the Prince-individual has nothing to do with some individualism of moral conscience or power, or the aestheticism of panache. While it is the attribute of an individual, *virtù* is not the *intrinsic essence* of individuality; it is merely the reflection, as conscious and responsible as possible, of the objective conditions for accomplishment of the historical task of the hour in a Prince-individual.

Once we have defined the form of existence of the Prince-individual, understood that he is not a private citizen, and grasped the exceptional *position* entailing that in his case *virtù* governs the use of vice and virtue in the accomplishment of his historical task, we must examine the structure or 'organic composition' of this public personage. We need to know how he acts, what the principles of his political practice are.

The mechanism of the Prince is set out in Chapter XVIII, in connection with the issue of 'How rulers should keep their promises'. It is no accident, says Machiavelli, that the ancients made the Centaur the political teacher of their great men, suggesting that rulers should become like this strange being: half-man, half-beast. In fact, the Prince must have a dual nature. Why? Because there are two ways of contending: 'one by using laws, the other, force. The first is appropriate for men, the second for animals; but because the former is often ineffective, one must have recourse to the latter. Therefore a ruler must know well how to imitate beasts as well as employing properly human means.'[35] We are on familiar territory: the state's political practice must combine force (animal) and consent (human). But let us examine this more closely.

What does it mean to employ human means? It means to govern 'by laws' (which we shall construe as moral laws), in respecting the moral laws of kindness, fidelity, generosity, keeping one's word, and so on.[36] It is thereby specified that in order to obtain the people's consent, it is indispensable to practise the moral virtues, which act on attitudes by their prestige and their recognition, without any violence. But when the laws are impotent, one must also be able to resort to force, employ animal means. This is the other aspect of the Prince. Here it is no longer a matter of moral virtue, but of violence, whose result alone counts, as we know, 'because one should reproach a man who is violent in order to ruin things, not one who is so in order to set them aright'.[37] Employment of force is foreign to morality: it is the converse of the use of legal means. It then seems as if we have exhausted the issue. There are two types of practice, and they are *conjointly* necessary: 'a ruler needs to use both natures . . . and one without the other is not effective'.[38]

However, there is a considerable surprise in store for us. For the animal that is intended to represent *force*, just as man was intended to represent laws, *is divided in two*. The Prince who is to imitate beasts must take two animals, not one, as models – the lion and the fox: 'One needs . . . to be a fox to recognise traps, and a lion to frighten away wolves.'[39] On pages 68–9 the meaning of this dual personality is specified. The lion is 'very fierce', while the fox is 'very cunning'. The context leaves no room for doubt: to be a fox is to be the *master of fraud* – both the fraud played on you, so that you can recognize its traps, and the fraud you must be able to perform, so as to entrap others. It is to be the master of guile and deception – not only in acts of war, traps, feints, and so on, but in the government of men generally. Now what is astonishing in this division, this dual personality, of the beast is precisely that *the beast*, which is force, is divided into force (the lion) and fraud (the fox); whereas fraud – the art of deception – apparently has nothing to do with force, is not a division of force, but something quite different. What? To answer this question, some details are required.

First of all, we can say this: there are not two ways of governing men – by laws and by force – but three – by laws, force and fraud. But as soon as this statement has been made, we realize that fraud is not a mode of government like the others; it is not on the same level. Laws *exist* – let us say as human institutions, recognized rules, and opinions; force exists – let us say as the army. In contrast, however, fraud possesses no objective existence: it does not exist. If fraud is a way of governing, given that it has no existence, it can be employed only when it is based on laws or force. Fraud, then, is not a third form of government; *it is government to the second degree, a manner of governing the other two forms of government*: force and laws. When it utilizes the army, fraud is stratagem; when it utilizes laws, it is political guile. Fraud thus opens up a space, beyond force and laws, for diverting their existence – a space in which force and law are substituted for, feigned, deformed,

and circumvented. Mastery of fraud in the Prince is the distance
that allows him to play at will on the existence of force and
laws, to exploit and, in the strongest sense of the word, feign
them.

Let us leave aside the cunning use of force, of which Machiavelli gives countless examples in connection with war strata-
gems, and stick to laws. They are indeed the most important
thing. The chapter where Machiavelli discusses the Centaur, the
Prince who is both man and beast, opens with these words:
'Everyone knows how praiseworthy it is for a ruler to keep his
promises, and live uprightly [hence according to the law] and
not by trickery.' The opposition laws (morals)/deception is
blatant here. Machiavelli adds: 'Nevertheless, experience shows
that in our times the rulers who have done great things are those
who have set little store by keeping their word, being skilful
rather in cunningly deceiving men.'[40] The opposition laws/
deception thus discloses two limit-cases: that of the Prince
who governs exclusively by laws (moral virtue: good faith,
kindness, and so on); and that of the Prince who governs by
deception, tricking men's minds. The first is laudable. What of
the second?

The opposition laws/deception contains precisely the answer
to this question. Deception is counterposed to laws as immorality
to morality. To engage in trickery with the law is, in effect, to
'get around' people; it is to 'load the dice' by lies and deception.
We now understand why Machiavelli assigns fraud to the category of the animal, rather than the human. To employ human
means is to exercise the moral virtues; to play the fox is to
exercise a non-violent violence, the vice of all vices: untrust-
worthiness, deceit. And we then grasp why fraud, an animal
faculty aligned with force on account of its immorality, is paired
with laws as their opposite, and is a form of government to the
second degree: in effect, it is the capacity to govern government
by laws immorally; it is the art of affecting to abide by laws
while violating or circumventing them. It is the necessity and
understanding of non-being under the guise of being, and vice
versa.[41]

However, this whole line of argument, correct as it is, is
meaningful only if its *presupposition* is clarified: namely, the
existence of laws and government by laws, in the sense this

expression has in Chapter XVIII of *The Prince*, where laws designate moral laws, the moral virtues. In order to be able to engage in trickery with the laws, they must first *exist*, be acknowledged, and be such that they cannot be ignored. Here we rejoin the problem of the Prince's representation in popular opinion.

When we said that the foundation of the New Principality by the New Prince had to ignore every actually existing form, this meant every existing *political* form. For wherever he establishes himself, the New Prince will encounter men who possess their own customs and obey religious and moral laws: in short, men subject to representations, opinions, or what might anachronistically be called ideologies. It is not a matter of such and such an individual's opinion, but of the opinion of the mass, of what Machiavelli calls '*il volgo*': 'the common people are the vast majority, and the few are isolated when the majority and the government are at one'.[42] What individuals might do in a private capacity – for example, flout religious or moral law, get round its proscriptions to satisfy their passions or ambition – is of little concern. Even when they violate the law, they proclaim and acknowledge it; the acknowledged law is there to be transgressed. Moreover, Machiavelli basically considers that the majority of the people, *il volgo*, abide by the law: the little men, who comprise the vast majority, desire only the security of their goods and persons, and especially their womenfolk. It is the small minority that is motivated by passion and ambition for power, and will stop at nothing to satisfy them.

Such is the reality that dominates everything in this domain: the existence of a mass religious and moral ideology. The implication is obvious: to achieve his national and popular goals, the Prince must start out by respecting the people's ideology, even – especially – if he wants to transform it. He must take care that every political act, each form of political practice, intervenes and resonates as a matter of fact in the element of this ideology. He must therefore take charge of it, accept responsibility for the ideological effects of his own political practice, anticipate them, and inscribe them in it. And since the Prince is literally the public face of the state, he must take care that the people's representation of his figure is inscribed in popular ideology, so as to produce effects beneficial to his politics. For this representation plays a key role in the state's constitution, in the association of subjects and their education.

Now, it is here that fraud comes in, and in the first instance because it *can*. It can intervene because the people are so disposed that they trust appearances more than reality:

> [M]ost men judge more by their eyes than by their hands. For everyone is capable of seeing you, but few can touch you. Everyone can see what you appear to be, whereas few have experience of what you really are; and those few will not dare to challenge the popular view. . . .[43]

That men believe in appearances was already inherent in their attachment to the obvious facts of religion, rites of worship, true or false miracles, as to the self-evidence of customs and morality. It follows that nothing is easier than deceiving them: 'men are so naive, and so much dominated by immediate needs, that a skilful deceiver always finds plenty of people who will let themselves be deceived'.[44] Of all the possible deceptions, there is one that interests the Prince: the deception *par excellence* that holds out to men the very appearance they believe in, that they recognize, that they recognize themselves in – let us say, in which their ideology recognizes itself in them – namely, moral and religious laws.

We thus return to the relation between deception and laws, and, before that, to the relation between moral virtues and *virtù*. Machiavelli's precept that fraud 'should be well concealed: one must be a great feigner and dissembler', falls under a more general precept: that the Prince must know how not to be good. To appreciate the necessity of fraud, we must revert to the Prince's historical task, the exceptional situation imposed on him, the means he is compelled to employ, and his *virtù*. If we might consider the two extremes of his practice, we find, on the one hand, that he must be good and virtuous so far as is feasible; and on the other, that he must learn not to be good, and thus to do evil. But even when he is reduced to this extremity, the Prince must, if he can (and it is not always possible), 'disguise' his immoral conduct as moral conduct, feigning virtue:

> A ruler . . . need not actually possess all the above-named qualities, but he must certainly seem to. Indeed, I shall be so bold as to say that having and always cultivating them is harmful, whereas seem-

ing to have them is useful; for instance, to seem merciful, trust-
worthy, humane, upright and devout, and also to be so. But if it
becomes necessary to refrain, you must be prepared to act in the
opposite way, and be capable of doing it.[45]

Thus we see how, through the ideological representation of
his figure, the Prince's ideological policy must be determined. It
may be characterized by saying that this ideological policy must
be subject to the primacy of politics *tout court*. The Prince must
take the reality of popular ideology into account, and inscribe
therein his own representation, which is the public face of the
state. But his ideological policy must be a politics, not an
ideological demagogy. There is no question of the Prince con-
forming to the spontaneous ideology of the people in every
detail of his conduct and practice. He must compose, and
politically control, his conduct and its representation. At one
extreme, he must know that there are 'vices that enable him to
rule',[46] such as being cruel at the state's inception ('a new ruler,
in particular, cannot avoid being considered harsh'[47]); or being
mean at each and every opportunity.[48] And it is not a matter of
disguising these vices as virtues, for to use deception would be
a political mistake, since in this instance it is the reputation for
cruelty and meanness that is politically operative. At the other
extreme, he must be apprised that there are *virtues that enable
him to rule*: mercy, trustworthiness, humanity, uprightness, piety.
These must be either possessed or affected, because their reputation is politically operative. But he must not ensnare himself in
them, or be bound to them, because necessity might demand
their renunciation. Politics is in command in everything; as a
function of its goal, it dictates the selection of political vices and
virtues alike, and their affectation when required.

The objective is to establish a correct ideological *relation*
between Prince and people, via the representation of the figure
of the Prince. As always, Machiavelli proceeds by examining
extremes: on one side, hatred and contempt; on the other, love.
He completely rules out the first extreme: the Prince must at all
costs avoid being hated and scorned. If he were hated, he would
be in the condition of a tyrant, at the mercy of popular rebellion;
if he were scorned, he would not be a ruler, but at the mercy of
the nobility's insurrection. Let us translate: *the Prince must not at*

any price find himself in the position of having the people against him.
But what of love? Is it not the fondest wish of a popular ruler?
Machiavelli rejects this, too – albeit in more moderate terms – as
incapable of guaranteeing stable relations between Prince and
people on its own. For love is inconstant: 'whether men bear
affection depends on themselves'.[49] 'While you benefit them,'
Machiavelli writes, 'they are all devoted to you: they would shed
their blood for you; they offer you their possessions, their lives,
and their sons . . . when the need to do so is far off. But when
you are hardpressed, they turn away.'[50] A more reliable bond
must be found: *fear.* In Chapter XVII of *The Prince*, Machiavelli
writes:

> A controversy has arisen about this: whether it is better to be loved
> than feared or vice versa. My view is that it is desirable to be both
> loved and feared; but it is difficult to achieve both and, if one of
> them has to be lacking, it is much safer to be feared than loved.[51]

The advantage of fear is that it persists ('fear is sustained by a
dread of punishment that is always effective'). But it persists
because it is the creation of the Prince, who controls its cause –
something that is not the case with love: 'whether men bear
affection depends on themselves, but whether they are afraid
will depend on what the ruler does. A wise ruler should rely on
what is under his control, not on what is under the control of
others.'[52] If the results of these two analyses are compared, we
see the relation between Prince and people settled in the following definition:[53] 'it is perfectly possible to be feared without
incurring hatred'.[54]

This formula – fear without hatred – might seem harsh for the
people of a popular Prince. But to give it its precise meaning, it
must be developed. That the Prince must at all costs avoid being
hated by his people obviously signifies that he must beware of
alienating the people as the greatest peril. But there is more:
hatred in Machiavelli has a precise connotation. Above all, it is
the people's hatred of the *nobles*. In connection with the kingdom
of France, for instance, we are told that Louis IX 'was well aware
of the ambition and arrogance of the nobles. . . . On the other
hand, . . . he knew that the people hated the nobles.' The founder
of the kingdom therefore established the *parlement* 'to restrain
the nobles and favour the people'.[55] Hatred thus possesses a

class signification. In the formula 'fear without hatred', the phrase 'without hatred' signifies that the Prince demarcates himself from the nobles and sides with the people against them.

But there is still more: fear without hatred closes down one space and opens up another, specific space: the minimal political base from which the people's friendship – an expression Machiavelli prefers to the people's love – becomes the decisive political objective. In effect, what is ruled out is the people's undiluted love, without coercion, since it is precarious and capricious. What is aimed at instead is the people's friendship, 'popular goodwill'[56] on the basis of state coercion. Machiavelli constantly returns to this theme, which gives explicit expression to his own position. Take, for example, Cesare Borgia:

> [T]he Duke had established a very good basis for his power, because he controlled all the Romagna, together with the Duchy of Urbino and . . . he thought that he had secured the *friendship* of the Romagna, and that he had *won over* all the inhabitants, for they had begun to enjoy prosperity.[57]

A further twenty examples could be cited that leave no room for doubt. The theory of fear without hatred is the theory of the political precondition for 'popular goodwill' towards the Prince. It is also, factually, an acknowledgement of the popular state's double function: the unity of coercion and popular consent that so struck Gramsci in Machiavelli.

Finally, to appreciate this policy of 'fear without hatred' properly, it must be called by its name: it is *an ideological politics*, politics in ideology. It must also be remembered that this representation of the Prince's figure in the people, on the basis of religion, accounts for only one *component* of the means of state power, the other component comprising the army. It must be remembered that of the two the dominant means is the army, whose role in the unification, formation and constitution of the people as a people we have observed. Finally, it must be recalled that state ideology and force alike are subordinate as means to one and the same end: the constitution of a new, popular state that must face up to its historical task: unifying Italy.

Let us go back a little further. If we consider the Italian situation of extreme misery and depletion, we observe that: (1) Italy is a 'matter' awaiting only a suitable form to unify it; but

(2) on the other hand, nothing is to be expected of the political forms it is decked out in and cursed with, because they are all old, feudal forms. That is why the Prince must be completely new, and begin to execute his historical task starting out from a completely new principality. This involves creating a political base. While it must be completely new, and sweep away the old political forms, this political base (which must be a popular political base in the sense in which we have subsequently learnt to refer to a popular base) is not going to be constituted in a vacuum. The Prince will have to 'mould' existing men, who bear the scars of feudal forms of political domination, in their customs, and their religious and moral laws. Once again, Machiavelli's political objective is not to reform the constitution of a state, or even to take power in the formal framework of an existing state, but to constitute a radically new *political* base. This base must be imposed by force for it to be capable of existing; it must be expanded by force to be capable of enduring; it must fell all the wretched Italian states one after the other, and be defended by force against foreign states. In these conditions we can appreciate why the army is the quintessential instrument of state power – not only of the exercise of state power, but of the state's very existence; and why it is assigned the preponderant role – not only military, but also political and ideological – since it is the crucible of the people's political and ideological unity, the training school of the people, the becoming-people of the people.

We then appreciate the political nature of that strange relation of people to Prince: fear without hatred. It is indispensable to the constitution of the New Principality, which has to be popular if it is to resist assaults from without and wrest the means of building the national state from the old states; it is indispensable to the education of the populations of conquered principalities and republics. If the Prince knows how to inspire fear without hatred in his subjects, he guarantees himself the time required for his grand design, and will be able to win over populations acquired by war or guile. But there again, this is only a beginning. For fear without hatred is simply the means to an end that surpasses it: the ideological base from which 'popular goodwill' will, little by little, be won.

A final word. If fear without hatred is indeed such, we can

see that it is the mandatory resolution of a political problem linking the constitution of the national state to a twofold imperative: that the Prince's absolute power is 'popular' (not that the people are in power, but that out of fear initially, and then friendship, they recognize themselves in the Prince's popular politics and in his figure); and that by means of his power the popular Prince circumscribes the class struggle between nobles and people, to the advantage of the latter. Utopia? But it suffices to know the history of the constitution of national states in broad outline to appreciate that Machiavelli does nothing but *think* the conditions of existence, and the class conditions, for that form of transition between feudalism and capitalism which is *absolute monarchy*.

Machiavelli is not in the least utopian: he simply thinks the conjunctural *case* of the thing, and goes *dietro alla verità effettuale della cosa*. He asserts it in concepts which are *philosophical* and no doubt make him, in his temerity, solitude, and scorn for the philosophers of the tradition, the greatest materialist philosopher in history – the equal of Spinoza, who declared him *'acutissimus'*, most acute. Spinoza considered him *acutissimus* in politics. He would appear not to have suspected that Machiavelli was also most incisive in materialist philosophy. I shall attempt to demonstrate this in a subsequent work.[58]

Notes

For full details of the English editions of *The Prince* and the *Discourses on Livy* used, see Editorial Note, p. ix.

Foreword

1. There are two other versions of this Foreword. The first begins exactly like Althusser's *Montesquieu: Politics and History* ('I make no claim to say anything new about Montesquieu'): 'I make no claim to say anything new about Machiavelli, especially after the very penetrating thesis devoted to him by Claude Lefort in France.' [E]
2. Claude Lefort, *Le Travail de l'œuvre: Machiavel*, Éditions Gallimard, Paris 1972. [E]
3. Francesco De Sanctis, *Storia della letteratura italiana* (Feltrinelli, Milan 1956, p. 106): 'ti colpisce d'improvviso et ti fa pensoso'. In a letter of 25 July 1962 to Hélène Rytman, Althusser wrote that he had 'just bought' this work. [E]

Chapter 1

1. Niccolò Machiavelli, *The Art of War*, Bk III, in *The Chief Works and Others*, vol. 2, trans. Allan Gilbert, Duke University Press, Durham, NC, 1965 p. 640; trans. altered. [E]
2. 'A Note on Machiavelli', in Maurice Merleau-Ponty, *Signs*, trans. Richard C. McCleary, Northwestern University Press, Evanston, IL, 1964, pp. 211, 218.
3. 'Probabilmente la questione del Machiavelli resterà una di quelle che non si chiuderanno mai e non passeranno agli archivi': 'La Questione del Machiavelli', in Benedetto Croce, *Indagini su Hegel e schiarimenti filosofici*, Laterza, Bari 1952, p. 176. [E]
4. 'Preface to Autograph Manuscript', *Discourses*, p. 15.
5. 'Dedicatory Letter', *The Prince*, p. 34.
6. *The Prince*, ch. XV, p. 54; trans. altered.
7. 'Among the principal causes Aristotle gives for the downfall of tyrants is the one of having injured others through women by raping them, violating them, or breaking up marriages': *Discourses*, Bk III, ch. 26, p. 319. [E]

8. 'The German Constitution', in *Hegel's Political Writings*, trans. T. M. Knox, Clarendon Press, Oxford 1964, pp. 143–242. [E]

9. See especially Antonio Gramsci, *Selections from the Prison Notebooks*, ed. and trans. Quintin Hoare and Geoffrey Nowell Smith, Lawrence & Wishart, London 1971, Pt II, ch. 1, 'The Modern Prince', pp. 125–43. [E]

10. *The Prince*, ch. III, p. 8.

11. Montesquieu, Preface to *The Spirit of the Laws*, trans. and ed. Anne M. Cohler *et al.*, Cambridge University Press, Cambridge 1989, p. xliii; emphasis added. [E]

12. Ibid., Bk I, ch. 1, p. 3; emphasis added. [E]

13. From this point to the end of *Machiavelli and Us*, Louis Althusser works on the basis of the first, corrected version of his course, making numerous handwritten additions and corrections to the text (see Editorial Note, p. viii). The indicated revisions will simply be designated 'late handwritten correction' or 'late handwritten addendum'. However, the handwriting and content of some of these revisions allow us to date them as almost certainly 1986. When this is the case, we shall so specify, it being understood that other modifications may likewise date from the same period. A faulty link has prompted us to restore a passage excised by the author here: it is indicated in square brackets. [E]

14. The words 'case', 'hence' and 'singular' are late handwritten addenda. [E]

15. 'Aleatory, singular case' is a late handwritten addendum. [E]

16. 'Its case' is a late handwritten addendum. [E]

17. 'The case of' is a late handwritten addendum. [E]

18. 'In fact, by their aleatory future' is a late handwritten addendum. [E]

19. 'Uneven development' is a late handwritten addendum; 'difference' a late handwritten correction, replacing 'contradiction'. [E]

20. Cesare Borgia, Duke of Valentinois, second son of Pope Alexander VI. See *The Prince*, ch. VII, p. 28: 'Everything would have been easy for him, if he had been well when Alexander died.' [E]

21. See René Descartes, *Meditations on First Philosophy*, II, in *Selected Philosophical Writings*, trans. John Cotttingham *et al.*, Cambridge University Press, Cambridge 1988, p. 80. [E]

22. To take up a famous remark – dangerous if misconstrued – if 'the truth is revolutionary', it is in the sense of truth as defined by Lenin: 'truth is always concrete', realized in concrete forces, *actual*; and it is effective because it is actual. It remains the case that the term 'truth' [*vérité*] is ideological and that one should speak, as does Spinoza, of the *true* [*vrai*]. [The last sentence is a handwritten addendum to the note, itself handwritten. (E)]

23. 'Dedicatory Letter', *The Prince*, p. 4; emphasis added.

24. *Selections from the Prison Notebooks*, p. 126. [E]

25. Ibid., pp. 125–7:

> Machiavelli's *Prince* could be studied as an historical exemplification of the Sorelian myth – i.e. of a political ideology expressed neither in the form of a cold utopia nor as learned theorising, but rather by a creation of concrete phantasy which acts on a dispersed and shattered people to arouse and organise its collective will. The utopian character of *The Prince* lies in the fact that the Prince had no real historical existence; he did not present himself immediately and objectively to the Italian people, but was a pure theoretical abstraction – a symbol of the leader and ideal *condottiere*. However, in a dramatic movement of great effect, the elements of myth and passion which occur throughout the book are drawn together and

brought to life in the conclusion, in the invocation of a prince who 'really exists'. Throughout the book, Machiavelli discusses what the Prince must be like if he is to lead a people to found a new State; the argument is developed with rigorous logic, and with scientific detachment. In the conclusion, Machiavelli merges with the people, becomes the people; not, however, with some 'generic' people, but the people whom he, Machiavelli, has convinced by the preceding argument – the people whose consciousness and whose expression he becomes and feels himself to be, with whom he feels identified. The entire 'logical' argument now appears as nothing other than auto-reflection on the part of the people – an inner reasoning worked out in the popular consciousness, whose conclusion is a cry of passionate urgency. The passion, from discussion of itself, becomes once again 'emotion', fever, fanatical desire for action. This is why the epilogue of *The Prince* is not something extrinsic, tacked on, rhetorical, but has to be understood as a necessary element of the work – indeed as the element which gives the entire work its true colour, and makes it a kind of 'political manifesto'.

26. See the *Communist Manifesto*, section III, 'Socialist and Communist Literature', which begins with 'Reactionary Socialism' ('feudal socialism', 'petty-bourgeois socialism', and 'German or "true" socialism'), proceeds to 'Conservative or Bourgeois Socialism', and concludes with 'Critical-Utopian Socialism and Communism'. Section IV discusses the 'position of the communists in relation to the various existing opposition parties'. ('Manifesto of the Communist Party', in Marx, *The Revolutions of 1848*, Penguin/NLR edition, Harmondsworth 1973, pp. 62–98, esp. pp. 87–98).
27. 'Aleatory' is a late handwritten addendum. [E]
28. See the entry on 'Machiavellianism' in the *Encyclopédie*:

> Few works have made such a stir as the treatise on *The Prince*: the reason is that it teaches rulers to trample on religion, the rules of justice, the sanctity of treaties, and everything sacred, when self-interest demands it. Chapters XV and XXV might be entitled: 'Circumstances in which it suits the Prince to be a villain'.

29. The following handwritten passage occurs in the margin of the typed text: 'are of interest only as retorts to others (favourable to Machiavelli despite this diabolical side to him); behind Machiavelli there always lurks a battle of which he is the symbolic/imaginary focus'. [E]
30. Rousseau, *The Social Contract*, Bk III, ch. 6, in *The Social Contract and Discourses*, trans. G.D.H. Cole, Everyman, Dent, London 1993, pp. 244–5. [E]

Chapter 2

1. 'Niccolò Machiavelli to Zanobi Buondelmonti and Cosimo Rucellai, Greetings', *Discourses*, p. 14; emphasis added.
2. Dedicatory Letter, *The Prince*, p. 3; trans. altered and emphasis added.
3. Preface to Autograph Manuscript, *Discourses*, p. 16; trans. altered.
4. Ibid.; trans. altered.
5. Ibid.
6. *Discourses*, Bk I, ch. 39, p. 105.

7. *Discourses*, Preface to Bk II, p. 150.
8. 'Theoretical status' is a handwritten correction, replacing 'scientific emptiness'. [E]
9. 'Between "cases" ' is a late handwritten addendum. [E]
10. 'Or, rather, their "invariants" ' is a late handwritten addendum. [E]
11. *Discourses*, Bk I, ch. 6, p. 37.
12. *The Prince*, ch. XXV, pp. 84–5.
13. *The Prince*, ch. XVIII, p. 62.
14. 'Or, rather, *"aleatory"* ' is a late handwritten addendum. [E]
15. See *Discourses*, Bk I, ch. 2, pp. 22–8.
16. 'Ontology' is a late handwritten correction, replacing 'theory'. [E]
17. 'Juridical and political' is a late handwritten correction. [E]
18. *Discourses*, Bk I, ch. 2, p. 26.
19. Ibid.; trans. altered and emphasis added.
20. Ibid.; trans. altered.
21. 'Aleatory' is a late handwritten addendum. [E]
22. Whereas, for Marx, hazard or chance is always objective. [This note is a late handwritten addendum. (E)]
23. 'Into the void' is a late handwritten addendum. [E]
24. 'Aleatory' is a late handwritten addendum. [E]
25. Preface to Bk 2, *Discourses*, p. 150.
26. Ibid.; trans. altered.
27. Preface to 1531 Roman Edition, *Discourses*, p. 17.
28. Ibid.; emphasis added.
29. 'Wholly positive and affirmative' is a late handwritten addendum, probably intended to replace a previous handwritten addition ('definite') which was not excised by the author. [E]
30. *The Prince*, ch. II, p. 6.
31. Edmond Barincou, editorial note in Machiavelli, *Œuvres complètes*, Bibliothèque de la Pléiade, p. 1497.
32. See *Discourses*, Bk I, ch. 2, p. 27. Immediately after the theory of the cycle, we have the examples of Sparta – 800 years! – Athens (many fewer), and then Rome. *Founded by kings*: 'Romulus and all the other kings passed many good laws suitable to living in liberty.' Rome's 'early institutions, even if defective, did not, none the less, deviate from the straight path which could lead them to perfection'. When the kings were expelled and two annual consuls established, 'those who drove them out … *drove out of Rome only the title of king and not kingly power*' (emphasis added). The task of the rest of Roman history was to perfect this government, to make it a *combination of the three powers*: '[S]ince that republic had only the consuls and the senate, it came to be nothing more than a mixture of two of the three elements mentioned above, that is, the [monarchy] and the aristocracy. It remained only for the city to give way to popular government: once the Roman nobility became insolent … the people rose up against it.' The nobility had to concede a share of its power, with the institution of the tribunes: 'In this manner the creation of the tribunes of the plebeians came about, after which the condition of the republic became more stable, since all three forms of government had their roles.' An extraordinary republic! – composed of royal power (without the title), or the consuls; noble power, or the senate; and popular power, or the tribunes – a combination of three powers that 'created a perfect republic'. The proof of this perfection is that Rome escaped the law of the cycle; it cancelled it because Rome's monarchical character was successfully preserved. 'And fortune', Machiavelli writes,

was so favourable to Rome that although this city passed from a government of kings and aristocrats to a government of the people, through the
same steps and for the same reasons that were discussed above, *the kingly
authority none the less was never entirely abolished* to give authority to the
aristocrats, nor was the authority of the aristocrats completely diminished
in order to give it to the people, but *since this authority remained mixed, it
created a perfect republic.* (Trans. altered and emphasis added)

33. 'The Eighteenth Brumaire of Louis Bonaparte', in Marx, *Surveys from Exile*,
    Penguin/NLR, Harmondsworth 1973, p. 149.
34. Ibid., pp. 147–8; trans. altered.
35. See Albert Mathiez, *La Vie chère et le mouvement social sous la Terreur*, Éditions
    Payot, Paris 1927 (1977 reprint, vol. 1, p. 49): 'Behind the affluent Third Estate
    the famished and fierce Fourth Estate rose on the horizon.' [E]
36. 'The Eighteenth Brumaire', p. 148.
37. 'Intellectual *power*' is a late handwritten addendum. [E]
38. 'The Eighteenth Brumaire', p. 149.
39. 'Presents his "case"' and 'solely as proof that his theory of the aleatory
    invariant is *true*' are late handwritten addenda. [E]
40. 'Because aleatory' is a late handwritten addendum. [E]

Chapter 3

1. Francesco De Sanctis, *Storia della letteratura italiana*, Feltrinelli, Milan 1956,
   vol. 2, pp. 104–6.
2. *Discourses*, Bk I, ch. 12, p. 55; emphasis added.
3. *The Prince*, ch. XXVI, p. 87.
4. 'Hence emptiness' is a late handwritten addendum. [E]
5. *The Prince*, ch. XXVI, p. 88; emphasis added.
6. Ibid., pp. 90–91.
7. Ibid., p. 89.
8. Ibid.
9. Dante, *The Divine Comedy, Inferno*, Canto I, ll. 100–102: 'Many are the
   creatures with whom she [the beast] mates and there will yet be more, until
   the hound comes that shall bring her to miserable death' (Sinclair translation,
   Oxford University Press, New York 1981, p. 27). See Jacqueline Risset's note
   on these lines in her edition of *La Divine Comédie* (Flammarion, Paris 1985):

   The allegorical meaning is that of a providential saviour who will restore
   justice and peace on earth. Commentators have identified him with various
   historical figures, in particular Can Grande della Scala, who received Dante
   in exile in Verona, and to whom *Paradiso* is dedicated; and Henry VII,
   Emperor of Germany, whom Dante admired and who was due to be
   crowned in Rome (but died before reaching there, in 1313). [E]

10. *The Prince*, ch. VI, p. 19.
11. Ibid.
12. *The Prince*, ch. III, p. 6.
13. *Discourses*, Bk I, ch. 1, p. 20.
14. 'The void once again' is a late handwritten addendum. [E]
15. *Discourses*, Bk I, ch. 1, p. 21.
16. *Discourses*, Bk I, ch. 3, p. 28.
17. *Discourses*, Bk I, ch. 2, p. 22; trans. altered.

18. 'This invariant' is a late handwritten addendum. [E]
19. *Discourses*, Bk I, ch. 3, p. 28.
20. Ibid.
21. Ibid., pp. 28–9.
22. The inverted commas are a late handwritten addendum. [E]
23. *Discourses*, Bk I, ch. 7, p. 38.
24. *Discourses*, Bk I, ch. 4, p. 29.
25. Ibid., p. 30.
26. *The Prince*, ch. IX, p. 34.
27. *Discourses*, Bk I, ch. 16, p. 64.
28. *The Prince*, ch. IX, p. 35.
29. *Discourses*, Bk I, ch. 5, p. 31.
30. *Discourses*, Bk I, ch. 6, p. 34; trans. altered.
31. Ibid.
32. Ibid., p. 35.
33. Ibid., pp. 35–6.
34. Ibid., p. 36.
35. Ibid.
36. Ibid.
37. Ibid.; emphasis added.
38. Ibid., p. 38; emphasis added.
39. *Discourses*, Bk I, ch. 10, p. 48.
40. *Discourses*, Bk I, ch. 9, p. 45.
41. This sentence is a late handwritten addendum. [E]
42. *Discourses*, Bk I, ch. 9, p. 45.
43. Ibid.
44. Ibid.
45. This sentence is a late handwritten addendum. [E]
46. *Discourses*, Bk I, ch. 9, p. 45.
47. 'Not "nothingness", but emptiness' is a late handwritten addition. [E]
48. *The Prince*, ch. II, p. 6.
49. See *The Prince*, ch. I, p. 5; emphasis added.
50. *The Prince*, ch. XI, p. 40.
51. See Augustin Renaudet, *Machiavel*, Éditions Gallimard, Paris 1956, ch. 2: 'The Political Problem in Machiavelli's Œuvre'. A heavily annotated copy of Renaudet's work was found in Althusser's library. [E]
52. *The Prince*, ch. III, pp. 6–7; trans. altered.
53. Ibid., p. 8; emphasis added.
54. Ibid.
55. Ibid.
56. Ibid.
57. *The Prince*, ch. VI, p. 19.
58. Ibid.
59. Ibid.; trans. altered.
60. Ibid., p. 20.
61. *The Prince*, ch. VII, p. 23.
62. Ibid.
63. Ibid.
64. Ibid., p. 28
65. Cesare Borgia died on 12 March 1507 while fighting in front of the castle of Viarra. [E]
66. Late handwritten correction, replacing 'the dialectic of the political practice'. [E]
67. This sentence is a late handwritten addendum. [E]

68. In the margin of the two preceding sentences we find the following hand-written annotations: 'that it is necessary to know how to handle the abstraction/(the two ends of the abstraction)/(the suspense of Machiavelli)'. [E]

Chapter 4

1. Antonio Gramsci, *Selections from the Prison Notebooks*, ed. and trans. Quintin Hoare and Geoffrey Nowell Smith, Lawrence & Wishart, London 1971, p. 263. See, in particular, Louis Althusser, 'Marx dans ses limites', in *Écrits philosophiques et politiques. Tome I*, Éditions Stock/IMEC, Paris 1994, pp. 500–12. [E]
2. 'Material' is a late handwritten addendum. [E]
3. *The Prince*, ch. VI, p. 21.
4. 'State apparatus' is a late handwritten addendum. [E]
5. *The Prince*, ch. VI, p. 21.
6. These formulas derive from Clausewitz and Mao, respectively. [E]
7. See *Discourses*, Bk II, ch. 10, p. 177: 'Wealth is not, contrary to popular opinion, the sinews of warfare.' [E]
8. See *The Prince*, ch. XX, p. 75: 'the best fortress a ruler can have is not to be hated by the people'. [E]
9. See *Discourses*, Bk II, ch. 17, p. 195: 'How much value should armies in the present day place on artillery; and if the generally held opinion about artillery is true.' [E]
10. *The Prince*, ch. XIII, p. 49.
11. *The Prince*, ch. XII, p. 44.
12. Ibid., p. 43.
13. Ibid.
14. *The Prince*, ch. XIII, p. 49.
15. 'Sequence of events' is a late handwritten correction, replacing 'dialectic'. [E]
16. *The Prince*, ch. XIII, p. 48.
17. Ibid., pp. 49, 50.
18. Ibid., p. 50.
19. Ibid.; emphasis added.
20. Ibid., p. 49; emphasis added.
21. In the margin of the two preceding sentences we find the following hand-written annotation: 'reverse order'. [E]
22. *The Prince*, ch. XIII, p. 51.
23. *Selections from the Prison Notebooks*, p. 132.
24. 'Material' is a late handwritten addendum. [E]
25. *The Prince*, ch. XVIII, p. 63.
26. 'Factual' is a late handwritten addendum. [E]
27. *Discourses*, Bk I, ch. 11, p. 50; trans. altered and emphasis added.
28. Ibid., p. 52.
29. *Discourses*, Bk I, ch. 12, p. 54.
30. Ibid., p. 55.
31. 'Ideological' is a handwritten addendum present in the earliest version of the text. [E]
32. *The Prince*, ch. XV, p. 55.
33. *The Prince*, ch. VIII, p. 31.
34. Ibid., p. 33.
35. *The Prince*, ch. XVIII, p. 61.
36. Ibid.

37. *Discourses*, Bk I, ch. 9, p. 45; emphasis added.
38. *The Prince*, ch. XVIII, p. 61.
39. Ibid.
40. Ibid.
41. This sentence is a late handwritten correction, probably dating from 1986. [E]
42. *The Prince*, ch. XVIII, p. 63.
43. Ibid.
44. Ibid., p. 62.
45. Ibid.
46. *The Prince*, ch. XVI, p. 57.
47. *The Prince*, ch. XVII, p. 58.
48. See *The Prince*, ch. XVI, p. 57.
49. *The Prince*, ch. XVII, p. 60.
50. Ibid., p. 59.
51. Ibid.
52. Ibid., pp. 60–61.
53. Ibid., p. 59.
54. The following handwritten note occurs here: 'Go, and I do not hate you!' [E]
55. *The Prince*, ch. XIX, p. 66.
56. Ibid., p. 65.
57. *The Prince*, ch. VII, p. 26; trans. altered and emphasis added.
58. This paragraph is a late handwritten addendum, almost certainly written in 1986. [E]

Appendix

Machiavelli's Solitude

First of all, allow me to thank the Association Française de Science Politique and Jean Charlot for the great honour they have done me in inviting me to this exchange. And I should also express to you straight away a first scruple I have about this invitation. Your Association is primarily interested in the major political issues of the present day, whereas I have proposed a subject which may perhaps be judged to lack actuality: Machiavelli. Moreover, and this is my second scruple, you are used to hearing either well-known political figures, or historians, or political scientists. But I am only a philosopher, and it is as a philosopher that I want to approach with you what I have called Machiavelli's solitude. To tell you that I am a mere philosopher is to say that there are many questions I should find it very hard to answer, but I hope you will forgive me this if I manage at least to make myself clear about the few points I wish to raise. I hope that, despite the difference of our formations, competences, and interests, an exchange will be possible, an exchange from which, personally, I have great expectations.

I know that it is customary in your Association that the guest speaker replies to questions that have been communicated to him in advance. I believe the lack of actuality and slightly offbeat character of my subject must have inhibited my interlocutors. For I have only received three questions. One of these, from Pierre Favre, concerns the epistemological conceptions I have outlined in essays which are already rather old. He will permit me to reserve this question for a private conversation, because it is too personal and would take me too far from my subject. The second question, from Colette Ysmal, concerns Gramsci's assessment of Machiavelli: yes, I do think, as Gramsci did, that Machiavelli is a theoretician of the national state, and hence of absolute monarchy as a transitional state between feudalism and capitalism, but I believe he is so under very exceptional conditions, which I will discuss later. The third question, from Hugues Portelli, concerns the relationship between Machiavelli's thought and the Marxist tradition: yes, I do think there is such a relationship, but it seems to be one of coincidence and repetition, rather than one of direct descent. I may also be discussing this point.

With your permission, I should therefore like to begin the discussion with a few reflections on my chosen theme: Machiavelli's solitude.

It cannot but be objected that it is paradoxical to talk of solitude vis-à-vis an author who has constantly haunted history, who, from the sixteenth century to the present day, *without interval*, has been ceaselessly either condemned as the devil, as the worst of cynics, or else practised by the greatest statesmen, or again praised for his daring and for the profundity of his thought (under the *Aufklärung*, the *Risorgimento*, by Gramsci, etc.). How can one claim to speak of Machiavelli's solitude when he is seen to be constantly surrounded in history by a vast crowd of irreconcilable opponents, supporters and attentive commentators?

Yet it is possible to speak of his solitude if only one notices the *division* Machiavelli's thought imposes on everyone who tries to deal with him. The fact that he so much divides his readers into supporters and opponents, and that despite changing historical circumstances, he continues so to divide them, shows how difficult it is *to assign him to one camp*, to classify him, to say who he is and what he thinks. His solitude first of all consists in this fact, that he seems *unclassifiable*, that he cannot be ranged in one camp alongside other thinkers, in one tradition, as other authors can be ranged in the Aristotelian tradition, or the tradition of natural law. No doubt it is also because of this *unclassifiability* that such different parties and such great authors have not succeeded either in condemning him or in adopting him without a part of him having eluded them, as if there were always something *unassimilable* in Machiavelli. If we set aside his partisans, if, from our present vantage point, we consider the *commentators* who have been working on his writings during the last century, we find something of this truth once again in their surprise. A moment ago I was talking of Machiavelli's thought. Now the great modern commentators have in fact adopted for themselves, but in a reflected way, as a component part of Machiavelli's thought, *one feature* capable of explaining the violent divisions which Machiavelli has aroused in history. His thought does indeed have all the appearances of a classical system of thought, one which proposes for itself an object, for example the prince, the difference species of principalities, the way to conquer and keep them, the way to govern them. To have all the appearances of a classical system of thought is to have all the appearances of a recognizable, identifiable and reassuring system of thought, all the appearances of a system of thought that can be understood unambiguously, even if it leaves unsolved problems. But almost all the commentators are in agreement that in Machiavelli we find something quite different from unsolved problems – *a riddle* – and that this riddle is, as it were, indecipherable. At the end of his life, Croce said that the Machiavelli question *would never be settled.* This riddle can take different forms, for example, the form of the well-known dilemma: is Machiavelli a monarchist or a republican? It can take subtler forms: how is it that his thought is both categorical and elusive? Why, as Claude Lefort has brilliantly demonstrated in his thesis, does it unfold via interruptions, digressions, unresolved contradictions? How is it that a system of thought apparently under such tight control is in fact both present and fleeting, complete and incomplete in its very manner of expression? All these disconcerting arguments support the notion that Machiavelli's *solitude* lies in the *unwonted* character of his thought.

Not commentators alone, but also ordinary readers, can bear witness to this. Even today, anyone who opens *The Prince* or the *Discourses*, texts now 350 years old, is, as it were, struck by what Freud called a strange familiarity, an *Unheimlichkeit*. Without our understanding why, we find these old texts addressing us as if they were of our own day, gripping us as if, in some sense, they had been written for us, and to tell us something which concerns us directly, without our exactly knowing why. De Sanctis noted this strange feeling in the nineteenth century when he said of Machiavelli that *'he takes us by surprise, and leaves us pensive'.*

Why this seizure? Why this surprise? Why pensive? Because his thought goes on inside us, despite ourselves. Why pensive? Because this thought can go on inside us only if it disturbs what we think, having taken us by surprise. As a thought that is infinitesimally close to us, and yet which we have never hitherto met, and that has over us the surprising power to take us aback. By what are we taken aback?

We are taken aback not by an ordinary discovery, the discovery of the supposed founder of modern political science, the man who treated politics, as Horkheimer states, for example, in the later Galilean manner, seeking to establish the variations of elements united in a constant relationship, thus treating it in the positive mode of *'that is how things are'* and *'here are the laws'* that govern the government of states.

No, it is not a discovery of this kind that takes us aback, for in so far as this discovery has passed into our culture and propagated itself in a whole scientific tradition, it is familiar to us, and can in no way surprise us, 'take us by surprise'. And yet Machiavelli himself proclaimed himself the inventor of a new form of knowledge, in the manner of all the great political explorers, as Vico and Montesquieu were to do: but this form of knowledge is precisely quite different from Galileo's, and his thought has remained, as it were, without succession, isolated in the time and the individual that saw its birth and gave birth to it.

Here I am touching on a decisive point in the solitude and the unwonted character of Machiavelli. But before going on to this point, and in order to be able to do so, I should like to prove that it is first necessary to dissipate the classical form of the Machiavellian riddle.

This classical form can be stated as follows: Was Machiavelli in his heart of hearts a monarchist, as *The Prince* seems to suggest, or was he a republican, as the *Discourses on the First Decad of Titus Livy* seem to suggest? That is how the problem is generally posed. But to pose it in this way is to accept as self-evident *a prior classification of governments,* a classical typology of governments going back to Aristotle, which considers the different forms of government and their normality and pathology. But Machiavelli precisely refuses to accept or practise that typology, and does not require his reflections to define the essence of any given type of government. His purpose is quite different. It consists – as De Sanctis and, following him, Gramsci realized – not so much in theorizing the national state as it existed in France and Spain in his own lifetime in the form of absolute monarchy, but *in asking the political question of the preconditions of the foundation of a national state in a disunited country, in Italy*, prey to internecine divisions and invasions. Machiavelli asked this question *in radical, political terms*, that is, by observing that this political task, the construction of an Italian national state, could not be carried out by any of the existing states, whether governed by princes, or republics, or finally Papal States, for they were all *old*, or – to put it in modern terms – all still enmeshed in feudalism – even the free cities. Machiavelli asked this question in *radical terms* by stating that '*only a New Prince in a New Principality*' would be capable of carrying out this difficult task.

A New Prince in a New Principality: for a new prince in an old principality could not achieve anything, since it would keep him the prisoner of its oldness. I believe it is crucial to have a proper grasp of the political meaning of this rejection and the indeterminacy in which Machiavelli leaves his readers. It is clear that Machiavelli sought the prince of his hopes, but he shifted from prince to prince, and in the end knew he would never find him. He was convinced by the urgency of the task, by the political misery of Italy, by the quality of the Italian people, and the cries rising from all sides, that such a prince would be welcomed by popular accord, and he found pathetic accents to express this urgency. That it was necessary and possible had already been proved to him by Cesare Borgia's adventure: he had almost succeeded in founding a new state, but this was because he was nothing to start with, because he was the prince of no state, and hence not the prisoner of the old political forms of the state with which feudalism and the papacy had covered an Italy ravaged by invasions. Convinced by the urgency of the political task and of the means abounding in Italy, Machiavelli was also convinced that the prince to come *would have to be free of all feudal fetters*, and be able to undertake the task from scratch. That is why he speaks in general of 'the New Prince in a New Principality', in general, in the abstract, without naming anyone or any place. This anonymity is a way of denouncing all the existing princes, all the existing states, and of appealing to an unknown to constitute a new state, ultimately as Cesare Borgia had carved out his, starting from a fragment of a province that was not a state and which his father the Pope had given him for his amusement. If an unknown were thus to start from nothing, and if fortune favoured his *virtù*, then he might succeed, but only on condition that he founded a *new* state, a state capable of *lasting*, and a state capable of *growing*, that is, of unifying the whole of Italy, by conquest or other means. The whole much-debated question of whether Machiavelli was a monarchist or a republican is superseded in the face of this alternative, and can be illuminated starting from these preconditions. For to found a new state, says Machiavelli, one must 'be alone'; one must be alone to forge the armed forces indispensable for any politics, alone to issue the first laws, alone to lay and secure the 'foundations'.

This is the first moment of the state, one that is necessarily the work of a single man who rises from private individual to prince; it is thus, if you wish, the monarchist or dictatorial moment.

But this condition is not a sufficient one. For a state thus formed is monstrously fragile. It is prey to two dangers: its master may fall into tyranny, which is as execrable to Machiavelli as despotism was to be to Montesquieu, since tyranny unleashes popular hatred, resulting in the destruction of the prince – and it may be torn by internecine factions, leaving it at the mercy of an external attack.

Thus, once founded, it is essential that this state be able to last. To make this possible, the prince, who was alone in its foundation, must, as Machiavelli puts it, 'become many', and set up a system of laws protecting the people against the excesses of the nobles, and a 'composite' government (his term) in which the king, the people and the nobles are represented. This is the second moment, the moment of the rooting of power in the people, to be precise, in the contradictions of the struggle between the people and the nobles, for scandalously, in defiance of the established truths of his time, Machiavelli defends the notion that the conflict of humours, of the lean against the fat – in short, the class struggle – is absolutely indispensable to the strengthening and expansion of the state.

It can, if you like, be maintained that this second moment is Machiavelli's republican moment. But when you compare what he says about the advantages of the government of France and the formidable historical example of Rome, which presents the paradox of being a republic founded by a king and preserving monarchy in the institutions of the republic, it is clear that it is not possible to separate the monarchist and the republican in him, or rather, that the alternative of *these two positions* does not suit his mode of thought. For what he wants is not monarchy or republic, as such – what he wants is national unity, the constitution of a state capable of achieving national unity. Now, this constitution is first achieved in the form of an individuality, call him a king who is capable of founding a new state and making it durable and apt to grow by giving it a composite government and laws: a government that gives scope for the struggle of the popular classes, in which the king and the people are on the same side in order to strengthen the state and make it ready for its national mission. Such, I believe, is the profound originality of Machiavelli in this matter. He cannot be accurately described as a *theoretician of absolute monarchy* in the sense of a modern conception of political science. He does, of course, think in terms of absolute monarchy; he bases himself on the examples of Spain and France. I should rather say that he is a *theoretician of the political preconditions of the constitution of a national state*, the theoretician of the foundation of a new state under a new prince, the theoretician of the durability of this state; the theoretician of the strengthening and expansion of this state. This is a quite original position, since he does not think the *accomplished fact of absolute monarchies* or their mechanisms, but rather thinks *the fact to be accomplished*, what Gramsci called the 'having to be' of a national state to be founded, and under extraordinary conditions, since these are *the conditions of the absence of any political form appropriate to the production of this result*.

This brings me back to the unwonted character of Machiavelli's thought.

For the short sentence he was so fond of, that 'one must be alone to found a state', has a strange resonance in his work once one has understood its critical function. Why alone? One must be alone to be free to carry out the historical task of the constitution of the national state. In other words, one must *turn out*, in fortune and *virtù*, to be, as it were, *torn up by one's roots, cut off from them, irredeemably cut off* from the political forms of the world of Italy as it exists, since they are all old, all marked by feudalism, and nothing can be hoped for from them. The prince can be new only if he is endowed with this solitude, that is, this freedom to found the new state. I say *turn out* in fortune and *virtù* to be, as it were, torn away from all this past, its institutions, its mores and its ideas, *turn out*, since, paradoxically, Machiavelli, who seems, in the manifest content of his arguments, to appeal to the consciousness of his contemporaries, lays no store by the *coming to consciousness* of the individual. If the individual has *virtù*, this is not ultimately a matter of consciousness and will; if he has *virtù*, it is because he turns out to be possessed and seized by it. Machiavelli did not write a Treatise on the Passions, nor one on the Reform of the Understanding. For him, it is not consciousness but the coincidence of fortune and *virtù* that causes a particular individual to turn out to be cut off from the preconditions of the old world in order to lay the foundations of the new state. Yes indeed, this sentence does resonate strangely in Machiavelli's work. Just as he said 'one must be alone to found a new state', so I say Machiavelli had to be alone to write *The Prince* and the *Discourses*. Alone – that is, he had to turn out to be, as it were, cut off from the self-evident truths dominant in the old world, detached from its ideology, in order to have the freedom to found a new theory and to venture, like the navigators he mentions, into unknown waters.

This was indeed the case. In a period dominated by the great themes of Aristotelian political ideology, revised by the Christian tradition and by the idealism of the ambiguities of humanism, Machiavelli broke with all these dominant ideas. This rupture is not explicit, but it is all the more profound for that. Has attention been paid to the fact that in his works, where he constantly evokes antiquity, it is not the antiquity of letters, philosophy and arts, of medicine and law, which is current in all the intellectuals that Machiavelli invokes, but a *quite different antiquity*, one discussed by nobody else, the antiquity of political practice? Has sufficient attention been paid to the fact that in these works that speak constantly of the politics of the ancients, there are *hardly any references to the great political theoreticians of antiquity*, no discussion of Plato and Aristotle, Cicero and the Stoics? Has attention been paid to the fact that in these works there is no trace of the influence of the Christian political tradition or the idealism of the humanists? If it is evident that Machiavelli radically marks himself off from all this past, a past which nevertheless dominates his own time, have we paid attention to the discretion with which he does so: without fanfares? He just says that he preferred to appeal to the actual reality of *the* matter [*della cosa*] rather than to its imagination. He did not call the imagination he rejected by its name, but we know that in his day it bore some very great names. He surely did have to be alone to conceal his discovery as he did, and to remain silent as to the names of his opponents.

But this is not enough to explain the unwonted character of Machiavelli. The fact that he was alone in stating a new truth is not enough to leave him in his solitude. All the great inventors have become famous for us, and their reasons are now clear to us. But such is not the case with him.

Machiavelli is alone because he has *remained isolated*; he has remained isolated because, although there has been ceaseless fighting over his thought, *no one has thought in his thought*. And no one has done so for reasons pertaining to the nature of his thought, but also for reasons pertaining to the thought in which others thought after him. As everybody knows, from the seventeenth century on the bourgeoisie elaborated an impressive political philosophy, the philosophy of natural law, which blocked out everything else, naturally including Machiavelli. This philosophy was built up from notions deriving from legal ideology, from the rights of the individual as a subject, and it attempted to deduce theoretically the existence of positive law and the political state from the attributes that legal ideology confers on the human subject (liberty, equality, property). As compared with Machiavelli and his particular problem, this is quite another world of thought. But it is also quite another ideological and political world. For the number-one object and stake of the philosophy of natural law is absolute monarchy: whether the theoreticians want to give it a rightful basis (like Hobbes) or to refute it by right (like Locke and Rousseau), absolute monarchy is their starting point and their subject of discussion; it is what is at issue, be it its justification or its condemnation. Here the difference becomes glaring. Machiavelli does speak of the absolute monarchy to be found in France or Spain, but as an example and an argument *to help in dealing with a quite different object*: the constitution of a national state in Italy; he is therefore speaking of *a fact to be accomplished*. The theoreticians of natural law speak *in the accomplished fact, under the accomplished fact of absolute monarchy*. They ask questions of right because the fact is accomplished, because the fact is disputed or problematic and must therefore be founded by right, because the fact is established and its rightful status must be disputed. But in doing so they block out every other discourse about absolute monarchy and the state, and in particular Machiavelli's discourse, which no one ever thinks has any philosophical consequences, because Machiavelli at no point speaks the language of natural law.

This is perhaps the ultimate point in Machiavelli's solitude: the fact that he occupied a unique and precarious place in the history of political thought between a long moralizing, religious and idealist tradition of political thought, which he radically rejected, and the new tradition of the political philosophy of natural law, which was to submerge everything and in which the rising bourgeoisie found its self-image. Machiavelli's solitude lay in his having freed himself from the first tradition before the second submerged everything. Bourgeois ideologists have long situated themselves in this second tradition to tell, in the language of natural law, their fairy-tale history of the state, the history that begins with the state of nature and continues with the state of war, before pacifying itself in the social contract that gives birth to the state and positive law. A completely mythical history, but one that makes pleasant listening, because in the end it explains to those who live in the state that there is nothing horrific in its origins, only nature and law; that the state is nothing but law, is as pure as the law, and as this law is in human nature, what could be more humane than the state?

We are all familiar with Part VIII of the first volume of *Capital* in which Marx tackles so-called 'original accumulation' (usually translated as 'primitive accumulation'). In this original accumulation, the ideologists of capitalism told the edifying story of the rise of capital just as the philosophers of natural law told the story of the rise of the state. In the beginning there was an independent worker who worked so enthusiastically, intelligently and economically that he was able to save and then exchange. Seeing a poorer passer-by, he helped him by feeding him in exchange for his labour, a generosity which found its reward in that it enabled him to increase his acquisitions and help other unfortunates in the same way out of his increased goods. Hence the accumulation of capital: by labour, thrift and generosity. We know how Marx replied: with a story of pillage, theft, exaction, of the violent dispossession of the English peasantry, expelled from their lands, their farms destroyed so as to force them on to the streets, with a quite different story and one far more gripping than the moralizing platitudes of the ideologists of capitalism.

I would argue that, *mutatis mutandis*, Machiavelli responds rather in the same way to the edifying discourse maintained by the philosophers of natural law about the history of the state. I would go so far as to suggest that Machiavelli is perhaps one of the few witnesses to what I shall call *primitive political accumulation*, one of the few theoreticians of the beginnings of the national state. Instead of saying that the state is born of law and nature, he tells us how a state has to be born if it is to last and to be strong enough to become the state of a nation. He does not speak the language of law, he speaks the language of the armed force indispensable to the constitution of any state, he speaks the language of the necessary cruelty of the beginnings of the state, he speaks the language of a politics without religion that has to make use of religion at all costs, of a politics that has to be moral but has to be able not to be moral, of a politics that has to reject hatred but inspire fear, he speaks the language of the struggle between classes, and as for rights, laws and morality, he puts them in their proper, subordinate place. When we read him, however informed we may be about the violences of history, something in him grips us: a man who, even before all the ideologists blocked out reality with their stories, was capable not of living or tolerating, but of *thinking* the violence of the birth throes of the state. In doing so, Machiavelli casts a harsh light on the beginnings of our era: that of bourgeois societies. He casts a harsh light, too by his very utopianism, by the simultaneously necessary and unthinkable hypothesis that the new state could begin anywhere, *on the aleatory character of the formation of national states*. For us they are drawn on the map, as if for ever fixed in a destiny that always preceded them. For him, on the contrary, they are largely aleatory, their frontiers are not fixed, there have to be conquests, but how far? To the boundaries of languages or beyond? To the limits of their forces? We have forgotten all this. When we read him, we are gripped by him as by what we have forgotten, by that strange familiarity, as Freud called it, of something repressed.

Let me return to Machiavelli's unwonted character by evoking what is perhaps the most disconcerting thing about his discourse. A moment ago I signalled the effect of surprise that reading him provokes. Not just what does he mean? But also why does he argue in this way, so disconcertingly, moving from one chapter to the next without any visible necessity in the transition, interrupting a theme which has to be picked up again later, but transposed, and never finally dealt with, returning to questions, but without ever giving them answers in the expected form? Croce said that the Machiavelli question would never be settled: it might perhaps be advisable to *wonder whether it is not the type of question asked of him which cannot receive the answer that this type of question requires and expects*.

It has been too often said that Machiavelli was the founder of political science, and there have been many commentators who have been pleased to discover in him one of the first figures of modern positivity, along with those of Galilean physics and Cartesian analysis, illustrating in all sorts of domains a new *typical rationality*, that of the *positive science* by which the young bourgeois class acquired the ability to master nature in order to develop its productive forces. In taking this road, it is only too easy to find certain passages in Machiavelli's writings, certain forms of mental experiment, certain forms of generalization established to fix the variations of a relationship, to justify this point of view. For example, it can be said of *The Prince* that in it Machiavelli proceeds by the exhaustive listing of the different principalities, thus anticipating Descartes's rule of complete enumerations; it can be said that in the relations between *virtù* and fortune Machiavelli is establishing a kind of law analogous to those that mark the beginnings of modern physics, and so on, and that in general, if, as he says, he has abandoned the imagination to go straight to the actual truth of the matter, this is to proceed in the spirit of a new positive science that can arise and grow only on the absolute precondition of no longer taking appearances at their word.

But I believe that the attempt to attribute to him this discourse of pure positivity always fails in the face of a disconcerting lack, of the suspended character of his theses, and the interminable character of a thought that remains enigmatic. I believe Machiavelli has to be approached from a different direction, following thereby an intuition of Gramsci's.

Gramsci wrote that *The Prince* was a political manifesto. Now it is the peculiarity of a political manifesto, if the latter can be considered in its ideal model, that it is not a pure theoretical discourse, a pure positive treatise. This does not mean that theory is absent from a manifesto: if it contained no positive elements of knowledge, it would be no more than words in the wind. But a manifesto that is political, and thus wishes to have historical effects, must inscribe itself in a field quite different from that of pure knowledge: it must inscribe itself in the political conjuncture on which it wishes to act and subordinate itself entirely to the political practice induced by that conjuncture and the balance of forces that defines it. This might be said to be an utterly banal recommendation, but the question becomes seriously complicated when it is remarked that this inscription in the objective, external political conjuncture also has to be represented *inside the very text that practises it*, if the intention is to invite the reader of the text of the manifesto to relate to that conjuncture with a full awareness and to assess accurately the place the manifesto occupies in that conjuncture. In other words, for the manifesto to be truly political and realistic – materialistic – the theory that it states must not only be stated by the manifesto, but located by it in the social space into which it is intervening and which it thinks. One could show how this is the case with the *Communist Manifesto*: after giving a theory of the existing society, it locates the theory of the communists somewhere in that society, in the region of other socially active theories. Why this duplication and double envelopment? In order to locate in the historical conjuncture under analysis, in the space of the balance of forces analysed, the ideological place occupied by that theory. We are dealing here with a twofold intention: the intention to mark clearly the kind of effectiveness to be expected of the theory, which is thereby made subject to the conditions of existence of theory in the social system; and the intention to describe the sense of the theory by the position it occupies in class conflicts.

This is to state in abstract terms something that is rather simple and is implied by everything Marx wrote, and was well understood by Gramsci. I mean that if Machiavelli's thought is entirely subordinated to his reflection on the historical task of the constitution of a national state, if *The Prince* is presented as a manifesto, if Machiavelli – who knew from his own experience what political practice was, not only from having toured the embassies of Europe, advised princes, known Cesare Borgia, but also from having raised and organized troops in the Tuscan countryside – *if Machiavelli is taking political practice into consideration, then his thought cannot be presented in the simple guise of the positivity of a neutral space.* On the contrary, it is arguable that if Machiavelli's thought is disconcerting, it is because it assigns to the theoretical elements it is analysing a quite different dispositive from that of a simple statement of constant relations between things. This different dispositive is the one we see in *The Prince* and the *Discourses*, a dispositive constantly obsessed, not only with the variable preconditions of political practice and its aleatory character, but also with its position in the political conflicts and the necessity that I have just indicated to reinscribe the theoretical discourse in the political arena it discusses. That Machiavelli was perfectly aware of this exigency is evidenced by too many passages for me to quote them all. I will give only one, to be found in the dedication of *The Prince*:

> I hope it will not be considered presumptuous for a man of very low and humble condition to dare to discuss princely government, and to lay down rules about it. For those who draw maps place themselves on low ground, in order to understand the character of the mountains and other high points, and climb higher in order to understand the character of the plains. Likewise, one needs to be a ruler to understand properly the character of the people, and to be a man of the people to understand properly the character of rulers.[1]

If we remember that Machiavelli did not write a treatise on the people but, rather, one on the prince, and that he proclaims without shame, on the contrary, as a positive argument, his 'low and humble condition'; if we consider everything to be found in *The Prince* and the *Discourses* in the light of these claims, it is clear that Machiavelli speaks of the prince by locating himself as part of the people, that he calls wholeheartedly for, and thinks, the practice of a prince who will establish Italian unity from the standpoint of the *'popolare'*. From all these analyses, we know that to invoke the people is to invoke struggle, and this struggle is a class struggle between the people and the nobles, so it is to invite the prince to carry out his historical mission by gaining the people's friendship – that is, to speak plainly, an alliance with the people against the nobility, the feudatories Machiavelli very harshly condemned because they did not work.

This, among many other things, is what struck Gramsci in Machiavelli. He is one of the first to have related the unwonted character of *The Prince*, which he described as a kind of manifesto, a living and non-systematic discourse, to Machiavelli's political position and to his awareness of the political task he was advocating. I say *awareness* advisedly, for it was because he knew his own position in the Italian political struggle and took the consequences in what he wrote *that Machiavelli treated theory as he did treat it*, both as something which would cast light on the major social realities that dominated that struggle, and as a subordinate moment in that struggle, inscribed somewhere in that struggle. Somewhere: no more than he could say who would found the new state or in what place in Italy, Machiavelli could not say where his work would be inscribed in the Italian struggles. At least he knew that it was somewhere in the background, that it was no more than a piece of writing, which he too abandoned to the chance of an anonymous encounter.

This, perhaps, is his final solitude. He knew that if his thought contributed at all to the making of history, he would no longer be there. This intellectual did not believe that intellectuals make history. And he had said too much, via his utopia, about the beginnings of the bourgeois national state, not to be denounced by that history. Only another system of thought, close to his by its rejections and its position, might save him from his solitude: that of Marx and Gramsci.

Translated by Ben Brewster

Note

1. *The Prince*, p. 4.

Index

Radical Thinkers ▼

Theodor Adorno
In Search of Wagner,
Minima Moralia

Theodor Adorno et al.
Aesthetics and Politics

Giorgio Agamben
Infancy and History

Aijaz Ahmad
In Theory

Louis Althusser
For Marx,
Machiavelli and Us,
On Ideology,
Politics and History

Louis Althusser, Étienne Balibar
Reading Capital

Étienne Balibar
Race, Nation, Class,
Spinoza and Politics

Jean Baudrillard
Fragments,
Passwords,
The Perfect Crime,
The System of Objects,
The Transparency of Evil

Walter Benjamin
The Origin of German Tragic
Drama

Jeremy Bentham
The Panopticon Writings

Roy Bhaskar
A Realist Theory of Science

Norberto Bobbio
Liberalism and Democracy

Judith Butler
Contingency, Hegemony,
Universality

Simon Critchley
Ethics-Politics-Subjectivity

Guy Debord
Comments on the Society of
the Spectacle,
Panegyric

Jacques Derrida
The Politics of Friendship

Derrida et al.
Ghostly Demarcations

Peter Dews
Logics of Disintegration

Terry Eagleton
The Function of Criticism,
Walter Benjamin

Hal Foster
Design and Crime

André Gorz
Critique of Economic Reason

Fredric Jameson
Brecht and Method,
The Cultural Turn,
Late Marxism

Ernesto Laclau
Contingency, Hegemony,
Universality,
Emancipation(s)

Georg Lukács
Lenin

Herbert Marcuse
A Study on Authority

Franco Moretti
Signs Taken for Wonders

Chantal Mouffe
The Democratic Paradox,
The Return of the Political

Antonio Negri
The Political Descartes

Peter Osborne
The Politics of Time

Jacques Rancière
On the Shores of Politics

Gillian Rose
Hegel Contra Sociology

Jacqueline Rose
Sexuality in the Field of Vision

Kristin Ross
The Emergence of Social Space

Jean-Paul Sartre
Between Existentialism and
Marxism

Edward W. Soja
Postmodern Geographies

Sebastiano Tempanaro
Freudian Slip

Göran Therborn
What Does the Ruling Class
Do When It Rules?

Paul Virilio
Open Sky

Paul Virilio
The Information Bomb,
Strategy of Deception,
War and Cinema

Immanuel Wallerstein
Race, Nation, Class

Raymond Williams
Culture and Materialism,
Politics of Modernism

Slavoj Žižek
Contingency, Hegemony,
Universality,
For They Know Not What
They Do,
The Indivisible Remainder,
The Metastases of Enjoyment

Printed in the United States
by Baker & Taylor Publisher Services